RUNES IN SWEDEN

Sven B. F. Jansson

RUNES IN SWEDEN

Translation
PETER FOOTE

Photo
BENGT A. LUNDBERG

GIDLUNDS
ROYAL ACADEMY OF LETTERS, HISTORY AND ANTIQUITIES
CENTRAL BOARD OF NATIONAL ANTIQUITIES

© Sven B. F. Jansson 1987
Original title *Runinskrifter i Sverige*, AWE/Gebers 1963
Translated from Swedish by *Peter Foote*
Photographer *Bengt A. Lundberg*
First edition, second printing
Printed in Sweden by
Fälths tryckeri, Värnamo 1997

ISBN 91 7844 067 X

Contents

Foreword

In all about 3500 runic inscriptions are known from Swedish territory. Because of this unique wealth of material, they make an important contribution to our knowledge of early culture and society in Sweden. They are our oldest linguistic monuments and they provide much contemporary information of inestimable value. The inscriptions often permit us to draw significant conclusions relating to general cultural history.

This book presents a survey of the Swedish runic material, both in words and pictures. All photos were taken by Bengt A. Lundberg, photographer at The Central Board of National Antiquities and The Historical Museum, Stockholm. The text was translated into English by Professor Peter Foote of University College London.

A concise bibliography of the academic literature is given at the end of the book. It does not pretend to be comprehensive but the titles included will guide the interested reader to earlier works on subjects considered only in the most summary fashion in the following chapters.

It may finally be noted that forms cited as Old Norse (ON), or sometimes more distinctively as Old West Norse (OWN), are given in the spellings conventionally used for "classical" Icelandic.

Sven B.F. Jansson

THE PHOTOGRAPHER'S FOREWORD

Photographing runic inscriptions often poses more problems than casual consideration might deem possible. The twofold aim of producing an aesthetically satisfying picture, of a rune stone for example, while showing the inscribed surface itself as clearly as possible, was often achieved in the past by drastic retouching. The resulting illustrations were more than clear but less than truthful.

The photographs in this book are a departure from that tradition. Most of them view the object not simply as a source of information but, equally, as a unique monument in the Nordic landscape.

My hope in consequence is that these pictures reveal and record a number of Swedish runic inscriptions as they can be experienced at first hand, now in the mid-1980s, by visitors to their sites.

Bengt A. Lundberg

The oldest runic inscriptions

The origin of runes has long been a subject for speculation: it can be called a classic problem in runic research. But the lively and lengthy debate has led to no conclusive answer.

In very early times the runes were regarded as a gift from the gods. In Scandinavia, as elsewhere, the mysterious act of giving permanent form to ephemeral speech was ascribed to divine intervention. This is illustrated by the inscription on the seventh-century Noleby stone (Västergötland), where the carver refers to his runes as "derived from the gods". The same highflown epithet, alliterating with the word "runes", recurs in the inscription on the ninth-century Sparlösa stone, which enjoins the reader to interpret *runaʀ þaʀ ræginkundu*. This adjective (ON *reginkunnr* "of divine origin") is otherwise attested only once in the Norse world, in *Hávamál*. It is used of runes there as well:

> *þat er þá reynt,*
> *er þú at rúnum spyrr*
> *inum reginkunnum,*
> *þeim er gørðu ginnregin*
> *ok fáði fimbulþulr...*

"It is then tested when you ask about the runes derived from the gods, those which the ruling powers made and the mighty sage [Odin] painted..." According to Norse belief, it was Odin who discovered these mystic, potent signs.

Seventeenth-century workers in the field advanced some fantastic views on the genesis of runes, and in much later times too others have been propounded which may be safely transferred from the runological domain to that of the history of ideas and learning.

A few decades back it was generally thought that the problem of runic origins was by and large solved, but opinion is now once more divided and this old controversy again wide open. The problem now appears decidedly more complicated than it used to.

What can probably be said for certain is that runes were based on a southern

Man-made rune stones are now a natural element of the Swedish landscape.

European alphabet and that it was a form of classical script which was the foundation of this great cultural advance among Germanic peoples. On general and typological grounds it seems easiest to believe that runes were created in the second century of our era and were inspired by classical alphabet forms. To achieve a universally acceptable explanation we clearly need some new finds that can be securely dated. At present, the very sparse material available as a basis for discussion of where and when runes were invented gives ample scope for airy constructions.

The oldest runic inscriptions found in Sweden have been dated to the third century. Among them are the inscriptions on a spear-blade from Mos in Stenkyrka parish (Gotland) and a silver brooch from Gårdlösa (Skåne). Both

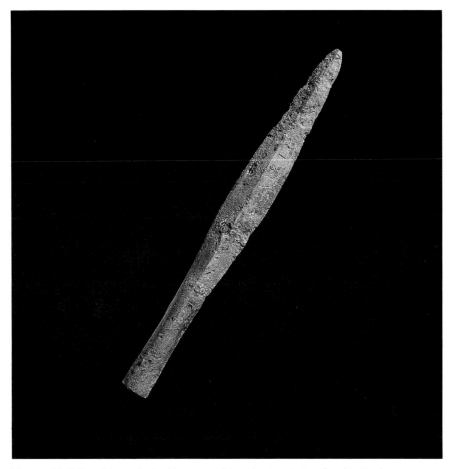

The spearblade from Mos on Gotland bears one of the oldest inscriptions found in Sweden.

objects are associated with graves dated by archaeological means. It is significant that these runes are scratched on metal objects of this kind, for it is on weapons and ornaments and suchlike that the oldest inscriptions have generally been preserved.

The Mos inscription is read *gaois* (or *sioag*), but what this sequence meant is impossible to decide. It may be the spear's name, or part of its name. Such uncertainty of interpretation is typical of the great majority of the inscriptions we possess from the first centuries of our era.

The runes on the Gårdlösa brooch probably contain the name of the writer—"I Unwod". His name means "the calm" (literally, "the unfrenzied").

The so-called Primitive Norse inscriptions are cut with runes belonging to the 24-character rune series, the system of script once employed by all

Germanic peoples, not only the North Germanic tribes but also those of the East and West Germanic branches.

The total number of inscriptions in this archaic runic series is over 200, of which some 50 have been found within the present-day borders of Sweden. It is probable that most of them, like the Mos inscription, will never be definitively interpreted. That is one reason why these earliest inscriptions of ours are treated so summarily in this book, although they deserve a much more detailed study both for their own sake and for the great interest they have from many other points of view.

Primitive Norse runes were used among the Swedes until some time towards AD 800, when they were superseded by a runic "alphabet" of only 16 characters. I shall return to this younger system below.

Objects from the Migration Age (*c.* 350–550) on which the whole Primitive Norse rune-row is recorded have thrice been found in Sweden. The oldest of them is on the stone found in 1903 on Kylver farm in Stånga parish (Gotland). The stone made a side-slab in a sarcophagus, dated on archaeological grounds to the fifth century, most probably to its first half. Incised on it in fine lines is a largely undamaged 24-character rune-row.

It should be noted that runes 4 **a** and 18 **b** in the Kylver series are "reversed runes". The general custom is for the side-strokes to be on the right hand of the stave (following the direction in which the runes were meant to be read). Further, rune 15 **ᛉ** has "collapsed"—usually the arms on it point upwards.

The Primitive Norse runic series is found on two gold bracteates, one from Vadstena, the other from Grumpan in Västergötland. Both were probably made about a century later than the Kylver stone. A third bracteate, found in the province of Närke (?), was clearly struck from the same die as the Vadstena bracteate. (The term "bracteate" is in this context reserved for small flat gold ornaments, worn suspended in some way, and with stamped or impressed decoration on one side only.)

One of the differences between the series on the Kylver stone and those on the bracteates is that in these the row is divided into three groups, so-called "families", each of eight runes. In later tradition they were called Frey's, Hagal's and Tyr's family respectively. It was a division which came to play an important part when runic ciphers were used (cf. p. 36 below).

In a normalised form the Primitive Norse futhark—so called from the opening characters—looked approximately like this:

f u þ a r k g w   **h n i j p ę ʀ s**   **t b e m l ng d o**

1 2 3 4 5 6 7 8   9 10 11 12 13 14 15 16   17 18 19 20 21 22 23 24

The Primitive Norse futhark.

The first thing to strike us is, of course, how completely different the order of the "letters" is from that of the classical alphabets—and consequently from our own. There have been several attempts to explain this remarkable lack of similarity but none has so far proved persuasive.

A question that calls for an answer is what purpose was served by the futharks cut on the Kylver stone and stamped on the gold bracteates from Vadstena, Närke (?) and Grumpan. It cannot be doubted but that the futhark, cut in the right sequence, was believed to confer powerful magic protection.

In the case of the Kylver stone it must be grave-magic at work: the inscription was after all made on the side of a stone coffin before it was buried in the ground. But there is more to it than just the futhark: an inspection of the other symbols

The stone from Kylver, Gotland, made a side-slab in a sarcophagus. On this stone the whole Primitive Norse rune-row is recorded.

Left: The gold bracteate from Vadstena in Östergötland has the Primitive Norse rone-row around the edge. *Right:* The runes on the Tjurkö bracteate were made by a man named Heldar.

incised on the stone bring out the magical purpose of the whole still more clearly.

Immediately after the last rune comes a sign which looks most like a simply-drawn fir-tree; and then higher up to the right are five runes **sueus**. The "fir-tree" must undoubtedly be interpreted as a **t**-rune with its "branches" six times repeated. To explain why an extra **t**-rune appears at this point and why it is furnished with so many "branches", I must go back to the futhark.

Each rune in the series had its own name, and by and large that name was the same throughout the extensive areas that shared a common Germanic culture. Each runic name began with the sound the character stood for—obviously for mnemotechnic reasons. Thus, the rune **h**, for example, was called "hail", **n** "need", **j** "year" (*jāra*, cf. German *Jahr*)—in the sense of "good season, crops", **s** "sun", **t** "Tyr" (a god's name), and so on. The rune **a** had the name *ansuʀ*, ON *óss*, *áss* (pl. *æsir*), "god".

Through their names both the **a**- and the **t**-rune are thus associated with divine powers, and it is significant that it is these two that we find most often in inscriptions of magic import. The name of the **t**-rune is that of the god Tyr, who was associated with war and success in war. This rune appears on the Kylver stone with sextuple branches—its magic power, its invocation of the god, has been magnified six times. We may compare the sixth-century Lindholm amulet (Skåne), which has an **a**-rune repeated eight times in a row, along with the **r**-, **n**- and **t**-runes each repeated thrice. The Sjælland bracteate offers a still more striking parallel, for its inscription ends with a triple-branched **t**-rune. It thus makes use of precisely the same method of intensification as on the Gotland

14

Kylver stone. On the Lindholm amulet the magic is reinforced by writing the whole rune three times. Information about this use of magic t-runes can be drawn from a different quarter. In the eddaic poem, *Sigrdrífumál*, a valkyrie imparts much handy runic lore to Sigurd the Dragon-slayer, Sigurðr Fáfnisbani. Among the stanzas is the well-known:

Sigrúnar þú skalt kunna,	"Victory runes you must know
ef þú vilt sigr hafa,	if you will have victory,
ok rísta á hialti hiǫrs,	and carve them on the sword's hilt,
sumar á véttrimum,	some on the grasp
sumar á valbǫstum,	and some on the inlay,
ok nefna tysvar Tý.	and name Tyr twice."

It was indubitably with magic intent that the isolated sequence **sueus** was also cut on the Kylver stone. We can find no intelligible meaning in it—it is an "abracadabra" word and like many such key-words it is a palindrome, reading the same backwards as it does forwards. It was a long time before such spellbinding formulas, used for mysterious ends, were treated as empty words.

Thus from start to finish the Kylver inscription was intended to bestow potent and effective protection. The carver had recourse to three related means: the futhark, the reinforced t-rune, and the magic word **sueus**. So much can be counted certain. What we cannot know for certain, on the other hand, is whether the carver intended to protect the grave and assist the dead amid the perils of the dark, or whether he meant to bind the dead man to his new home and prevent him from "walking", from coming back to interfere with the living and disturb their existence.

The gold bracteates were worn as jewellery; with their futharks they protected their wearers from misfortune. The Vadstena bracteate is like the Kylver stone in having a separate magical rune sequence.

Magic and sorcery occur remarkably often in the Primitive Norse inscriptions—one reason why they are so obscure. For we have the utmost difficulty in treading confident paths in this thick undergrowth, whose roots twine deep and round and through layers of cultural history millennia-old. In Primitive Norse times the rune-carvers were evidently often striving to gain power over the secret forces of nature. In various ways they sought to make contact with divine powers – to destroy an enemy, to find protection against disease and death, to defend the living from the dead and the dead from grave-robbers. With the help of runes they tried to make a spear never miss its mark, a man inviolable against weapons and a girl incapable of resisting his advances.

Still, we must make it clear that by no means all Primitive Norse inscriptions in Sweden serve the shadowy purposes of magic. The Tjurkö bracteate, for example, probably from the early sixth century, and found in 1817 not far from Karlskrona, has a different sort of message, at least in the main. An inscription which goes from right to left round the edge of it says: **wurte runoʀ an walhakurne heldaʀ kunimudiu.**

The start of the inscription, with verse rhythm and alliteration, is clearly artistically framed. The first word, **wurte,** is third sg. pret. of a weak verb *wurkian,* "make, produce, perform", Goth. *waurkjan,* ON *yrkia,* Sw. *yrka,* Engl. *work*; **wurte** (ON *orti*) alliterates with **walhakurne.** This is a compound whose second element is PN *kurna,* "corn, seed, grain", in the dat. sg. The first element is thought to contain a tribal name referring to Gauls or Celts or with a more general connotation of "southern people". This tribal name (OHG *Walh*) gave rise to OE *wælisc,* modern Engl. "Welsh", ON *valskr* "Gallic", Sw. *välsk.* An interpretation of the compound on the bracteate as "the Gallic (foreign?) grain" is thus possible. **an** immediately before it is of course prep. *an,* ON *á,* Engl. *on,* which takes the dat.

wurte runoʀ an walhakurne ought then literally to mean "made runes on the Gallic grain". The obscure last phrase would then seem to be a designation of the gold bracteate on which the runes have their place. The compound can be taken as a poetic periphrasis, a *kenning,* for "gold"—in that case, it is the earliest gold-kenning we know. In later centuries Norse scalds were to make constant reference to that coveted doomladen metal in ringing kennings: "billow's brightness", "dragon's bed", "seedcorn of Frode".

Everything suggests that **heldaʀ kunimudiu,** the inscription's last two words, are personal names. The first, an *a*-stem, is in the nom.; the second, a *u*-stem, in the dat. *Heldaʀ,* who has a name not otherwise attested, must be the man who "made" the runes on the bracteate. In **kunimudiu** (dat.) a nasal, *n*, is omitted before the the homorganic *d*; the nom. is PN *Kunimunduʀ.* This is a well-known name in West Germanic regions, found in sources as old as the sixth century (OE *Cynemund,* OHG *Chunimunt*).

The whole inscription on the Tjurkö bracteate can thus be read: "Heldar, for Kunimund, made the runes on the Gallic grain (= the gold pendant?)."

Of all the Primitive Norse inscriptions in Sweden, that on the Möjbro stone is by far the most famous. The inscription and the whole carving are different in kind from those so far considered. The Möjbro stone is an imposing monument, a rune stone set up to public view. It is on memorial stones of this sort that most of our runic inscriptions came to be preserved.

The Möjbro stone owes its fame not least to the skilful art of its unique pictorial addition. It is the high quality of this scene which explains why the stone figures more often than any other Swedish rune stone in works of reference of various kinds.

The stone was raised about AD 500 (perhaps earlier than that) at Möjbro in Hagby parish, southwest of Uppsala—that is, in the heart of the ancient realm of the Swedes. As far as we can tell, it was erected in memory of a dead chieftain. His name was **frawaradaʀ**, "the agile doer, the resourceful". Cf. ON *frár* "active, agile, quick"; *radaʀ* is nomen agentis from PN **rāðan,* ON *ráða* "prevail, decide, rule". The **d**-rune stands here for the voiced dental fricative *ð*.

The rider springing forward on his loose-reined horse dominates the Möjbro stone. He holds his shield in his left hand and brandishes his weapon in his right. Two animals run beside the horse. The whole scene has a rare living quality, everything caught in motion. It might well seem natural to regard the picture as a representation of the *Frawaradaʀ* named in the inscription. But that can hardly be the case. The impression the picture gives is rather of a classical representation of a cavalryman: we can imagine that it offers a glimpse of fruitful contact with late Roman culture in the Migration Age.

Since the Möjbro stone is reproduced in so many works, not all of them runological, it should perhaps be mentioned that several important details on it were only first observed some thirty years ago (in 1950). Neither the round shield with its central boss nor the two animals lower down on the stone had previously been noticed. Of the animal on the left, running just in front of the rider, von Friesen had made out only a couple of lines. They played some part in his interpretation of the carving, for he thought that these "right-angle lines ... could be thought to indicate the vanquished opponent". (The two "lines" he saw are actually part of the back and tail of the animal.) His view did not go unchallenged. W. Krause wrote, for example: "Die gekrümmten Linien links unten halte ich nicht für die Andeutung eines am Boden liegenden Gegners des Reiters, sondern für Darstellung des Geländes, etwa einer Bodenerhebung" (*Runeninschriften im älteren Futhark,* 1937, p. 149).

The inscription is in two lines and must be read from right to left, starting with the bottom line. In the top line there was no room for the last rune of all, so it is cut higher up again. It reads: **frawaradaʀ anahahaislaginaʀ**.

The latter part of the long sequence after the name *Frawaradaʀ* gives the words *is* [*s*]*laginaʀ*; the first is PN *is* —still the same in English; the second is undoubtedly nom. sg. masc. of the past part. of the PN verb **slahan* "strike, slay, hit". The **s**-rune can be read double, since it was found unnecessary to repeat a rune at the start of a word when it was the same as the last rune in the preceding word. There have been many energetic attempts to interpret the sequence **anahaha** but the sense remains uncertain.

Memorial stones set up in roughly the same period as the Möjbro stone are known from other parts of Sweden, but they lack pictures and their inscriptions usually consist simply of one or two personal names. On the Skärkind stone (Östergötland), for example, is the name **skiþaleubaʀ**, on the Berga stone (Södermanland) the woman's name **fino**, PN Finnō "Finna", and the man's name **saligastiʀ** Salgæstr; cf. the PN masculine names *Hlewagastiʀ* and *Ansugastiʀ*.

The Möjbro stone from Uppland is a memorial stone. It is famous bouth for its inscription and its unique pictorial addition.

A longer inscription occurs on the Rö stone from Otterö (Bohuslän). Like the Möjbro stone, it was probably raised in memory of a man killed in battle. The inscription, unfortunately damaged where the surface has weathered, is in four parallel lines. If we start with the second line from the right—as was possibly the carver's intention—we can read it like this: **swabaharjaʀ... sairawidaʀ stainawarijaʀ fahido ek hra-aʀ satido [s]tain[a].** "Swabaharjaʀ is treacherously slain (?). [I] Stainawarijaʀ cut. I Hra-aʀ set up the stone."

PN *Swabaharjaʀ* represents a name well known from West Germanic (e.g. OHG *Suabheri*). Its Old Icelandic form is *Svávarr*. Among others, the father of Garðarr, one of the first discoverers of Iceland, had this name. According to *Landnámabók*, he was Swedish: *Garðarr hét maðr, son Svávars hins svænska. Hann átti iarðir í Siólandi en var fœddr í Svíaríki* (Hauksbók).

The word **sairawidaʀ** is obscure. It has been read as the past part. of a PN verb *sarwijan* "capture, betray", but also as an otherwise unattested *sairawindaʀ* "wound-covered". (On the omission of **n** in such a position see p. 16 above.)

With one exception, the other words pose no problems. **stainawarijar** is the man's name that appears in Old Icelandic as *Steinarr*. **fahido** (older **faihido**) is first pers. sg. pret. of the verb *faihian* "paint, colour, write, cut" (ON *fá, fáði*). The fourth rune of **hra-aʀ**, the subject of the last sentence, is illegible because of damage. **satido** (ON *setta*, OSw. *sætte*) is first. sg. pret. of the verb *satjan* "set, put, place", and **staina** is of course acc. sg. of **stainaʀ** (ON *steinn*).

The inscriptions now cited represent classical Primitive Norse. In the sources it appears as a relatively uniform language and it provides us with the most antique form we know not only of Scandinavian but of any Germanic tongue.

On some seventh-century rune stones in south Sweden traces are apparent of the radical changes which the language (and runic writing) underwent in Scandinavia in the period between the Migration Age and the Viking Age. This time of transition, the seventh and eighth centuries, partly coincided with the culturally distinguished Vendel Period. The late Primitive Norse inscriptions of Istaby, Björketorp and Stentoften give an impression of incipient disintegration in what had at least appeared to be a firmly fixed language and a traditional and uniform writing system.

An interesting change in runic writing can be observed on the Istaby stone in Mjällby parish (Blekinge), a change which is illuminating in a number of ways and which may therefore merit a more detailed description.

As noted above, the name of the old j-rune was *jāra* "good season" (see p. 14). Now, the fact is that significant developments were beginning in Primitive Norse already in the sixth century. Initial *j* and *w*, for example, were lost and short vowels in final syllables were syncopated. A runic name like *jāra* was equally affected and came to be pronounced *ār*, cf. ON *ár*, Sw. *år* "year". Since the runic names were based on a mnemotechnic system (the name began with the sound represented by the rune), the system was upset by the loss of initial *j*. By analogy the old j-rune then came to be regarded as the sign for an *a*-sound. A contributory cause to the disappearance of the j-rune was naturally that the loss of initial *j* in speech meant a considerable reduction in the number of cases where a j-rune was needed at all. An **a**-rune (ᚠ), on the other hand, already existed in the futhark. Its name was PN *ansuʀ* (> *óss, áss*), a word, that is, beginning with a nasalised *a*-sound. Thanks to the pronunciation change two signs for *a* thus came into being, and in time it became the practice to restrict ᚠ to nasalised *a* and to use the old j-rune for the corresponding unnasalised sound. This distinction between nasalised and unnasalised *a* was to remain in runic writing for nearly 500 years—for the two runes with their different functions were adopted in the new 16-character futhark of the Viking Age. In transliterating late Primitive Norse texts we distinguish the unnasalised **a**-rune (i.e. the old j-rune) as ᴀ, the nasalised (i.e. the original **a**-rune) as **a**.

After this discussion of a detail in the development of runic script and the language it recorded, we can return to the Istaby stone. The new **a**-rune (ᴀ) there has the form ᚼ. The inscription is divided into three lines:

> **hAþuwulafʀ hAeruwulafiʀ**
> **Afatʀ hAriwulafa**
> **warAit runaʀ þAiAʀ**

As will be seen, the inscription has seven ᴀ-runes and seven **a**-runes. The stone was carved in the seventh century by a man who lived in the transition period between Primitive Norse times and the Viking Age: can we observe him making any systematic distinction in his use of the two runes? Let us make a closer inspection.

The second line contains two words, the first of them undoubtedly the prep. *aftʀ* "after, in memory of". The carver here uses the ᴀ-rune for the unnasalised *a*-sound and the **a**-rune for the svarabhakti between *f* and *t*. The second word in the line also contains both types. **hAriwulafa** is acc. of the well-known man's name *Hæriulf* (ON *Herjólfʀ* "host-wolf, war-wolf"). Again the ᴀ-rune stands for the unnasalised sound and the **a**-rune for the svarabhakti between *l* and *f*. But the **a**-rune (ᚠ) is also used for the final vowel in *-wulafa*. What quality shall we attribute to it? Since the name is in the acc. and must thus originally have ended in *-n*, we may conclude that the **a**-rune stands for nasalised *a* here as well. In the other parts of the inscription we also find that the carver makes consistent use of the ᴀ-rune for unnasalised *a* and the **a**-rune for the svarabhakti *a*.

We can thus confirm that the carver of the Istaby stone employed the two runes in different functions: ᴀ for unnasalised *a*, **a** partly for nasalised *a* and partly for the vowel sound he thought he heard between certain consonants. We may infer that in his language a marked distinction was audible between nasalised and unnasalised *a*, and that the svarabhakti sounded closer to the nasalised than to the unnasalised pronunciation.

It may be noted that the changes in form of prep. *aftʀ* (which we see takes the acc.) can be followed in our runic inscriptions. In the earlier part of the Viking Age (ninth century) it has the form *aft*, while in the eleventh century there are many—one can almost say innumerable—instances

The Istaby stone from Blekinge was carved in the transition period between the Primitive Norse period and the Viking Age.

of it in the form *at*. This *at* (with the acc.) "after" is thus to be distinguished from prep. *at* (with the dat., ON and OSw. *at*, Latin *ad*) "to, at, by" etc., a word etymologically identical with the infinitive marker *at*, Sw. *att*.

The Istaby inscription begins with a man's name in the nom., **haþuwulafʀ**. (In standard PN it would have been written **haþuwulfaʀ**.) It is a compound of *haþu-* (ON *hǫð* "battle, war"—only known in poetry) and *-wulfaʀ*, an *a*-stem with nom. ending *-ʀ* (ON *úlfr*, OSw. *ulver* "wolf"). The carver thus inserts a svarabhakti vowel between *l* and *f* but omits the weak-stressed stem-vowel *a* between *f* and *ʀ*: an example of syncope after the preceding long syllable. On the other hand, the stem-vowel *u* remains after the short syllable in *haþu*, as does also the initial *w* before *u* in the second element.

In thirteenth-century Icelandic the name *Haþuwulfaʀ* appears as *Hálfr* – a telling illustration of the radical changes in North Germanic in the period just before the Viking Age.

From a formal point of view, and from other aspects too, the sequence **haeruwulafiʀ** is also of interest. It is clearly the nom. of a masc. *ia*-stem and in apposition to **haþuwulafʀ**. It is formed from the name *Heruwulfaʀ* with the suffix *-ia-*, and if it had been cut a couple of centuries earlier, it would have appeared as *heruwulfijaʀ*; cf. **holtijaʀ** on the fifth-century Gallehus horn. In this case the suffix indicates descent and shows that *Haþuwulfʀ* ("battle-wolf") belongs to the kindred of *Heruwulfʀ* ("sword-wolf"—*heruʀ*, the first element, becomes ON *hiǫrr* m. "sword", with *u*-breaking).

The names on the Istaby stone admirably illustrate the naming customs in leading Germanic families of the Migration Age. The three names are compounded of two substantives, all with a notably warlike content. The first elements are words meaning "war-host", "battle" and "sword" respectively and each is completed by the word "wolf". These personal names are akin to kennings for "warrior": "war-host-wolf", "battle-wolf", "sword-wolf".

Finally, it should be observed that all the names begin with *h*-. They are thus examples of alliterating names with first-element variation. In this they represent a very widespread type of Migration Age personal nomenclature.

The third line of the inscription is on the left side of the stone. Its first word, **waʀait**, is third sg. pret. of the strong verb *wrītan* "write, inscribe, carve". (The form shows svarabhakti *a* between *w* and *r*.) **runaʀ** is acc. pl. of PN *runu* f. (ON *rún*, early OSw. *run*). It agrees completely with the pl. *runaʀ*, *rúnar* found in Viking Age and medieval sources. We find the older pl. form *runoʀ* on the Tjurkö bracteate (p. 16 above). The word *run* f. "rune" is thus an *ō*-stem. (Modern Sw. *runa* is a later form, first attested in the fifteenth century.) The last word of the inscription—**þaiaʀ**—is acc. pl. f. of the demonstrative *sa*, ON *sá* (f.

pl. *þaʀ*, ON *þær*, "those, these"—the spelling in the inscription can be explained as analogically affected by the pl. stem form *þai-*).

What the inscription says is thus: "Hådulv, Hjorulv's descendant, cut these runes in memory of Härjulv."

There has been some controversy about the order in which the lines should be read. Several scholars (including O. von Friesen) take the view that the reading should start with **AfatR hAriwulafa** and interpret this prepositional phrase as an elliptical clause with both subject and verb understood: "In memory of Härjulv [the stone is set up]. Halv [=Hådulv] Hjorulvsson cut these runes." The chief reason for their opinion is that the inscription otherwise appears to be at odds with PN and ON

The Björketorp rune stone from Blekinge is one of three imposing stones arranged in a triangle, forming one of the most impressive monuments in Sweden. The inscription talks about the secret of mighty and potent runes.

rules of word-order. It must however be said that the runic texts preserved from the PN period are inadequate to give us clear ideas about syntax in general and that no precise PN parallel exists to the type of ellipsis postulated in "In memory of Härjulv [the stone is set up]".

Three other rune stones from Blekinge show close affinity to the Istaby stone, those of Stentoften and Gummarp (Gammaltorp parish) and Björketorp (Listerby parish). True, they do not share the Istaby stone's frank avowal of its memorial status—their inscriptions are more obscure and menacing—but the runeforms and writing style are at once enough to show the close connections between them. And the most striking link of all is found in the reappearance of the names **haþuwolAfʀ** and **hariwolAfʀ** on the Stentoften stone. The first of these was once also to be found on the Gummarp stone—that stone was moved to Copenhagen in the seventeenth century and perished in the great fire of 1728 there. According to a drawing made in 1627, it was apparently inscribed **haþuwolAfA[ʀ] sate staba þria ᚠᚠᚠ** "Hådulv set three staves fff". The three *f*-runes must be ideographs. The name of the rune was *fehu* n., ON *fé* "goods, cattle, wealth". The thrice-carved *f*-rune was presumably intended to assist the Blekinge lord, Hådulv, to riches.

The Björketorp stone makes part of one of the most impressive monuments in Sweden—and one that most kindles the imagination. It consists of three imposing stones, arranged in a triangle. The one with runes on it, standing 4 m above ground-level, has an inscription which can be plausibly rendered as follows: "I hid here the secret of mighty runes, potent runes. Whoever breaks this monument shall always be tormented by sorcery. Treacherous death shall strike him. I prophesy destruction."

The same formula occurs in the curse called down on anyone who breaks the monument found on the Stentoften stone.

In these two inscriptions the carver is thus saying that he has here "concealed" powerful runes—*falh ek heðra ginnarunaʀ*. In all probability the expression must refer to the customs of an older age, when inscriptions conferring magical protection were literally concealed—underground, down in the grave itself. In that way the Björketorp and Stentoften stones are related to the Kylver coffin-slab.

Parallels to these curses on disturbers of graves are known from classical Greek and Roman funerary inscriptions. And a number of Viking Age inscriptions, especially in Denmark, are similarly designed to threaten and scare.

In many respects, and not surprisingly, traditions from the Migration Age can be seen to live on into the Viking Age, but nevertheless with the ninth century we get a strong impression that a new epoch has dawned in Scandinavia, the historical situation has changed. The early migrations of Germanic tribes were of a totally different character from the Scandinavian expansion of the Viking Age, and no real connection exists between them.

The 16-rune futhark

We have relatively few runic inscriptions from the centuries before the Viking Age, their language often hard to understand, their messages obscure. They cast only a fitful light in the darkness enshrouding that period. As we saw above, alteration in the form of runes can be observed and some vacillation in their use, the latter partly the result of the radical changes the language was then undergoing. These changes—which evidently took place with some rapidity—meant that the linguistic foundations of common North Germanic were shattered. New sounds came into being through mutation and breaking, and it must have been a difficult matter for a rune-writer to decide which of the now out-of-date 24-rune series was best fitted to represent a new sound or sound-variant of hitherto unknown quality. As the number of phonemes grew, the 24-rune futhark became inadequate for rendering current speech-sounds with any precision. The old rune series had done good service up to now, and for its time it was undeniably a very impressive creation. But adapting the writing system to meet the challenge of phonetic novelty presented problems difficult to solve. Either order had to be imposed on the disarray by increasing the number of characters or else the same rune had willy-nilly to be used for several considerably different sounds. Creation of a rune series capable of representing every sound, a sort of phonetic alphabet in runes, was doubtless beyond men's powers at the time. Nor would it have been very desirable, for a large number of runes would have been needed and inscriptions in such an alphabet would have severely taxed both writer and reader. It comes as no great surprise, therefore, to find that the problem was solved by a *simplification* and *reduction* of the 24-rune futhark.

About AD 800, at the outset of the Viking Age, we meet the 16-rune series. It appears then in two fully-developed variants. This younger futhark must undoubtedly be seen as the outcome of conscious reforms: it is hardly thinkable that any kind of "natural" evolution could have produced such a rigorous system.

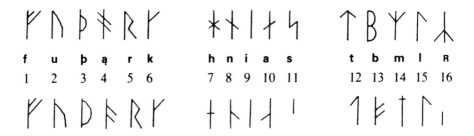

The two types of the Viking Age 16-rune futhark: normal runes and short-twig runes.

This 16-rune futhark has been found, over and over again, cut or scratched in complete or fragmentary form on many different objects. It often occurs on the walls of medieval churches. In many cases it was evidently inscribed with the same purpose as the 24-rune futhark on the Kylver stone and the Vadstena bracteate: people continued to put faith in the supernatural character of the runic series. During excavations in Novgorod (ON *Holmgarðr*; Holmgård) a piece of bone (from a pig) was found with the 16 runes of the new series inscribed on it; archaeologists date it to the first half of the eleventh century. There is a font in Övre Ullerud church in Värmland which has this futhark carved on it twice.

This Viking Age script is greatly simplified: from a linguistic point of view it is decidedly inferior to the 24-rune series, which in its time corresponded considerably better with phonetic realities. But the writer of it gained because the simplification spared him the need of making any close analysis of the sounds he wished to represent. It is a primitive form of writing but practical and convenient to use. It was easy for *the writer* to spell words in this new alphabet but not always easy for a reader to decide what was meant, for obviously some runes had to be used with a number of different sound-values. This was particularly true of the vowels. Scholars in the linguistic field may justifiably complain of the failure of the Viking Age writing system to convey any very precise impression of the phonemic complement of Viking Age speech.

In spite of everything, the Primitive Norse and the Viking Age futharks were intimately related: as is shown at once by the fact that the new series adopted no less than 10 of its 16 characters more or less unaltered from the older futhark.

As I mentioned, we meet the 16-rune futhark in two forms from the start. They have had a variety of designations in writings about runology. The one type has been called "ordinary" or "Danish runes"; the other type, which represents a somewhat simplified form of the first, has been referred to, with bewildering lack of uniformity, as "Swedish-Norwegian runes", "Rök runes", "short-twig runes" and "short runes".

These two types of the 16-rune series were used side by side but served different purposes. In several cases the "ordinary" runes have a more decorative form and they were consequently better suited for inscription on monuments of stone. That they have been counted more "ordinary" than others is simply because for us the "ordinary" place to find a runic inscription is precisely on a stone monument. This in turn naturally hinges on the fact that inscriptions on stone have lasted better than any on more perishable material. It is predominantly memorial inscriptions on stone that have remained for us to discover, but that does not justify the conclusion that runic writing was predominantly employed in this very limited function. A term like "ordinary runes" is inappropriate because it easily leads our thoughts in a wrong direction. It is unhistorical too, for in the eyes of their contemporaries the situation certainly appeared quite different.

As I said, the two forms of the 16-rune series served different purposes—and that explains the external differences between them. The "ordinary runes" have a more epigraphic character, the "Swedish-Norwegian runes" are simpler in shape and were undoubtedly chiefly used for recording matter of less ceremonious import. They were mainly cut in wood, not in stone—though, not surprisingly, we now know them mostly from stone-cut inscriptions. The demarcation between the functions of the two types was not rigid—nor of course is there any reason why we should expect it to be.

As for the names we should give the two types, it seems simpler and more perspicuous to distinguish between them on the basis of their different appearance. The so-called "Swedish-Norwegian runes" are undoubtedly a development, a simplified variant, of the so-called "ordinary runes". The difference between them chiefly lies in the fact that the former have shorter side-strokes, "twigs", than the monumental "ordinary runes", so a practical way of escaping the present terminological confusion is to adopt the old term, "short-twig runes", in place of "Swedish-Norwegian runes", and for want of anything better, to call the "ordinary" or "Danish" type, "normal runes".

The tendency towards simplification of the normal runes which we observe in the short-twig runes was completed in a radical way—very illuminating from the point of view of their use—in the so-called Hälsinge runes or "staveless runes". They can be called the "rapid writing" system of the Viking Age.

The reformer who created this kind of stenography on the basis of the short-twig runes was swayed by one fundamental principle. As far as possible, he dispensed with all the upright staves and left it to the "twigs" alone to indicate the sound represented by the symbol. The location of the marks, high, middle or low, decides how the runes are to be read. In the short-twig series the t-rune had the form ⑁ —it now becomes ´, an l-rune ⑁ becomes ‵ , an n-rune ⑁ becomes ‵ , and an a-rune ⑁ becomes ´ . The principle could not be put into practice in every case but as a whole the operation was a success. The complete series looks like this:

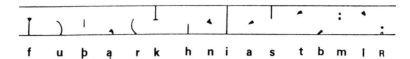

| f | u | þ | ą | r | k | h | n | i | a | s | t | b | m | l | R |

Staveless runes – the "rapid writing" system of the Viking Age.

The very existence of such a rapid writing system for everyday use permits us to conclude that people employed writing for various purposes and to a far greater extent than is commonly believed. There was need for a script that saved time and space.

It is obvious that this cuneiform-like script was not created for memorial inscriptions on stone monuments. On rune stones the characters look jumbled and agitated and far from decorative. They were meant for cutting in wood with a knife. That they have been preserved for our inspection on a few eleventh-century *stones* only means that in exceptional cases they stepped out of their proper everyday sphere.

As remarked in passing above, these runes have been called "Hälsinge runes" or "staveless runes". The name "Swedish runes" has also been proposed. The first name, "Hälsinge runes", has the weight of tradition behind it—given to them because they were once known only from inscriptions in Hälsingland (and Medelpad). Most of the inscriptions found in this individual script, and the longest of them, are still those of that northerly Swedish province, but again it seems more suitable to go by their appearance and prefer the term, "staveless runes". The name "Hälsinge runes" also suggests too narrow a regional limit, for we now have inscriptions in this futhark not only from Hälsingland and Medelpad but from Uppland and Södermanland as well. Inscriptions in "Hälsinge runes" cut in wood have recently come to light in Norway too, so the old term becomes still more misleading.

The names to be used here for the three varieties of the 16-rune futhark are consequently *normal runes, short-twig runes* and *staveless runes*. They at least have the advantage of neutrality. They are based on the forms of the runes, and their *forms* were after all conditioned by the different functions in which the three varieties were chiefly employed.

The fortuitously preserved inscriptions with staveless runes show that at least in Hälsingland, Medelpad and the central Swedish regions a need was felt already in the Viking Age for a quick, easy and economical script. This is a sure indication that quite extensive runic writing on wood was readily undertaken.

It ought to be emphasised that wood was by far the commonest material for runes, right from the beginning. It was this medium which dictated their form. Continental writers—Venantius Fortunatus in the sixth century, Hrabanus Maurus in the ninth—tell us that Germanic people cut runes on wooden boards, and Icelandic sources refer on several occasions to runes cut on sticks. Practically all these inscriptions have been lost—it is very sad, for example, that the rune-inscribed piece of wood found in the Kragehul bog on Fyn two hundred years ago is no longer with us, for if it were, we should then have a Primitive Norse inscription on the material for which runes were first intended. A lucky find of just such a piece was made in 1947 at Stenmagle on Sjælland, when a wooden box with a Primitive Norse inscription was excavated. The runes tell us who made the box. The excavations at Bryggen in Bergen have produced longer and shorter runic inscriptions on wood by the hundred, but they are all medieval in origin. All the same, it is of the utmost interest to see how varied these Bryggen inscriptions are: messages with a political content, business agreements and commercial contracts, verse in the old metres, menacing spells, prayers and private letters. A goodly number of inscriptions on wood have also been found in Sweden in recent decades, brought to light by excavation in medieval town-centres (Lödöse, Lund, Uppsala, Skara, Nyköping). In general, Swedish "medieval runology" has made considerable advances in recent years.

In connection with runes cut on wood, the Scandinavian word *bokstav* "letter" may be mentioned since it throws some light on the use of runes (cf. German *Buchstabe,* OE *bocstæf,* etc.). Its original meaning was a "stave"—a rune—cut on (a piece of) beechwood. The tree-name "beech" and the word "book" are thus properly one and the same. In a similar way, Latin *caudex, codex* originally meant "a piece of split wood", but later came to mean "document, book, manuscript" as well. In Sanskrit *bhūrja* means both a kind of "birch-tree" and "bark to write on".

Before we leave this summary account of the futharks and their uses and return to the inscriptions themselves, I shall just mention some forms which occur sporadically already in the late Viking Age. These are the so-called "dotted runes". They were created to help overcome the disadvantage of having to use a single rune to represent several different sounds. The need to expand the 16-rune futhark was thus felt at an early stage. An **i**-rune, for example, stood for at least three different vowels—*i, e, ä.* With a dot in the middle of the stave (᛫) a specific character for *e* (*æ*) was produced; in the same way a dot in the space between the main and subordinate staves of the **u**- and **k**-runes created specific characters for *y* (*ø*) and *g* (ᚼ, ᛈ).—The dotted rune system had a future in Sweden. Under the influence of the Latin alphabet it developed into a complete dotted rune alphabet with good resources for matching the changing sounds of speech. (Examples of medieval inscriptions in the dotted rune alphabet are given on pp. 164, 168 below.)

The Sparlösa stone is from the ninth century. It has carvings on all four sides, but as the runes are damaged in some important places the text is difficult to interpret. The pictures are mysterious too.

Runic inscriptions of the Viking Age

Like the transition centuries (*c.* AD 600—800) between the Primitive Norse period and the Viking Age, the first couple of hundred years of the Viking Age itself (*c.* 800—1000) have left us few rune stones. We are not however to believe that runic writing was then practised less extensively than in Primitive Norse times. All we can justifiably say is that in this epoch there was no great inclination to inscribe runic memorials on stone. It was not until the eleventh century that this custom became fashionable in Sweden. We can on the other hand safely assume that in the ninth century, when the two 16-rune futharks were developed, people made considerable use of runic writing. It is difficult to think that in this age of innovation, when the first townships were being established, there was any the less need for the art of writing than there had been previously. As far as we can see, the reason why we have so few inscriptions from the early Viking Age is simply because what was written was on materials that lacked the durability of stone (and metal). There are indications on the few rune stones preserved from this period that that was indeed the case.

To this early part of the Viking Age, the ninth century, poor in inscribed stones as it otherwise is, belong nevertheless two of Sweden's most remarkable and famous monuments: the Rök stone in Östergötland and the Sparlösa stone in Västergötland. The two stones are strikingly dissimilar. The Sparlösa stone is decorated with interesting pictures of an individual kind, which are as difficult to interpret as the runic inscription, unfortunately damaged in some important places. The Rök stone on the other hand is completely covered with runes, front, back, sides and top—no space has been given up to any other ornament.

The Rök stone is not only the most impressive monument ever raised in Sweden to commemorate a dead kinsman—it also stands as the great memorial of Swedish literature in antiquity. It is true that inscriptions in verse-form are already to be found in the Migration Age, chiefly in the potent language of sorcery, highly-wrought and archaically obscure, and it seems possible to glimpse a developed poetic art of magico-mythical character behind a number of Primitive Norse inscriptions. And later in the Viking Age we shall also meet rune carvers with some literary pretensions. But no inscription gives us such deep insight into the world of ancient literature as does the Rök stone. Some of the inscription is obscure; it reads thus:

Aft Væmoð standa runaʀ þar. En Varinn faði, faðiʀ, aft faigian sunu.

Sagum mogminni(?) þat, hværiaʀ valraubaʀ vaʀin tvaʀ þar, svað tvalf sinnum varin numnar at valraubu, baðaʀ saman a ymissum mannum.

Þat sagum annart, hvaʀ fur niu aldum an urði fiaru(?) meðr Hraiðgutum, auk do meðr hann umb sakaʀ.

> *Reð Þioðrikʀ*
> *hinn þurmoði,*
> *stilliʀ flutna,*
> *strandu Hraiðmaraʀ.*
> *Sitiʀ nu garuʀ*
> *a guta sinum,*
> *skialdi umb fatlaðʀ,*
> *skati Mæringa.*

Þat sagum tvalfta, hvar hæstʀ se Gunnaʀ etu vettvangi an, kunungaʀ tvaiʀ tigiʀ svað a liggia.

Þat sagum þrettaunda, hvariʀ tvaiʀ tigiʀ kunungaʀ satin at Siolundi fiagura vintur at fiagurum nampnum, burnir fiagurum brøðrum. Valkaʀ fim, Raðulfs syniʀ, Hraiðulfaʀ fim, Rugulfs syniʀ, Haislaʀ fim, Haruðs syniʀ, Gunnmundaʀ fim, Biarnaʀ syniʀ...

Nu'k minni meðr allu sagi. Ainhvaʀʀ...

Sagum mogminni þat, hvar Inguldinga vari guldinn at kvanar husli.

Sagum mogminni, hvaim se burinn niðʀ drængi. Vilinn es þat. Knua knatti iatun. Vilinn es þat...

Sagum mogminni: Þorr. Sibbi viavari ol nirøðʀ.

"In memory of Væmod stand these runes. And Varin wrote them, the father in memory of his dead son.

I tell the ancient tale which the two war-booties were, twelve times taken as war-booty, both together from man to man. This I tell second who nine generations ago lost his life with the Reidgoths; and he died with them, because of his offences.

> Theodric the bold,
> king of sea-warriors,
> ruled over
> Reid-sea shores.
> Now sits he armed
> on his Gothic horse,
> shield strapped,
> prince of Mærings.

The Rök stone was carved with short-twig runes. The beginning of the inscription at once gives the impression of artistically mannered prose.

That I tell the twelfth where the horse of Gunn [i.e. steed of the Valkyrie, the wolf] sees food on the battle-field, where twenty kings lie.

This I tell the thirteenth which twenty kings sat on Sjælland for four winters, with four names, born to four brothers: five Valkes, sons of Rådulv, five Reidulvs, sons of Rugulv, five Haisls, sons of Hord, five Gunnmunds, sons of Björn.

Now I tell the tales in full. Someone... [The stone is damaged here and decipherment and interpretation are uncertain.]

I tell the ancient tale which of the kinsmen of Ingvald was revenged by a wife's sacrifice.

I tell an ancient tale to which young warrior a kinsman is born. Vilin it is. He could crush a giant. Vilin it is.

I tell an ancient tale: Thor. Sibbe of Vi, ninety years of age, begot [a son]."

This unique inscription appears to contain many allusions to heroic lays and legends now lost. It thus gives us an insight into the literature that flourished at the beginning of the Viking Age. But a modern reader must sadly admit that these allusions in their compressed form can call up no associations that live for him. All or almost all of it is wrapped in oblivion. The literary milieu in which Varin incised his runes is not to be recovered. The tales and poems that were well known in Östergötland in the ninth century are inaccessible to us and doubtless always will be. And yet this cannot destroy the Rök stone's priceless value as a literary document.

The beginning of the inscription, with its alliteration and solemn rhythm, gives at once the impression of artistically mannered prose. Many poetic expres-

The crosses on the top of the Rök stone form a numerical cipher which depends on the division of the futhark into "families".

sions occur in the text, and in some places the word-order adopted is proper only to the elevated language of poetry.

The middle part of the inscription consists of a regular eight-line stanza in *fornyrðislag*, the narrative metre used in most of the eddaic poems. The stanza shows striking correspondences with the poetry familiar to us from early West Norse sources (cf. pp. 131–143 below on poetry in runic inscriptions).

Varin tests the reader's mental agility—and doubtless expects to stir admiration for his esoteric skills—by putting parts of his long text into different kinds of "secret" writing. Such coded lines make a partial frame for the rest of the text on the back of the monument and in these we can see that Varin had 24 in mind as a desirable number—the magic total of the runes in the old Primitive Norse futhark. The most striking line with cryptic runes is the one at the top of the back of the stone.

There we see three big diagonal crosses, whose arms towards the extremities are furnished with short strokes. Three more such crosses are on the stone's flat top. These crosses make a numerical cipher which depends on the division of the futhark into three "families" (see p. 12 above). In ciphers of this kind the "families" are counted from the end—the third, that is, as the first—so that the series appears as: 1. **tbmlR**, 2. **hnias**, 3. **fuþąrk**.

As well as the three crosses, the top surface also has five short-twig runes on it. The marks incised on the summit of the stone and at the top of the back look like this:

The cipher crosses of the Rök stone.

The strokes on the oblique line going down to the right give the number of the "family", those on the other diagonal give the number of the rune in the "family". If we start with the upper left of the first cross, we find two small strokes attached to it: they show it is "family" number 2. On the upper right arm are five strokes, so it is the fifth rune in that family we are to look for. We find that the fifth rune of the second "family" is **s**. In similar fashion the marks on the lower arms of the first cross lead us to the third rune of the second "family"— I. The two short-twig runes between the upper arms of the cross must now be included: the result is the well-known name, **sibi**, Sibbi, the hypocoristic form of *Sigbiorn*. Reading the second cross we first arrive at the

35

The Rök stone is not only the most impressive monument ever raised in Sweden to commemorate a dead kinsman, it also stands as a great memorial of Swedish literature in antiquity.

second rune of the third "family"— **u** —and once more the third rune of the second "family"— **i**. To them we must add the rune **a** cut between the upper arms of the cross. The third cross first gives the second rune of the third "family"— **u** again —and then the fourth rune of the second "family"— **a**. To these must be appended the **r** and **i** which come immediately after the cross and complete the inscription on the top face of the stone. The whole sequence concealed here is thus **sibi uiauari**. The top row on the back of the stone, deciphered in the same way, gives **ul nirupᴙ**, with the last two runes, **þ** and ᴙ (ı) placed in the lower "triangle" of the last cross, the one on the right.

This whole sequence in numerical cipher is thus to be read **sibiuiauari ulnirupᴙ** *Sibbi viavari ol nirǿþᴙ* "Sibbe of Vi, ninety years of age, begot [a son]".

The system which indicates a rune by the "family" it belongs to and its number in the "family" is found in several inscriptions, not least in Södermanland. The method by which the inscriber of the eleventh-century Rotbrunna stone (Uppland) gives his name is the same in principle. He ends with ‖""‖""‖‖""‖""‖‖""‖‖"""" + **hiuk**. The long lines give the "family", the short lines the number of the rune. We thus get "family" 2, rune 4 = **a,** "family" 2, rune 3 = **i**, "family" 3, rune 5 = **r**, "family" 2, rune 3 = **i**, "family" 3, rune 6 = **k**, "family" 3, rune 5 = **r**. So his name is **airikr** *Æirikᴙ* Erik. The verb form *hiogg* "cut", on the other hand, is in normal runes.

Immediately below the three large crosses on the back of the Rök stone we find an example of another kind of cipher, one making use of transposition. As the fig. on p. 35 shows, we have this line of short-twig runes: **airfbfrbnhnfinbant-fanhnu**. In this case each rune must be replaced by the one next following it in the 16-rune futhark. The outcome is **sakumukminiuaimsiburiniþ** *Sagum mogminni, hvaim se burinn nið*.

The same type of cipher remained long in use. It is found, for example, on the font in Kareby church (Bohuslän), where the font-mason cut his name in the sequence **orklaski**, which transposed gives **þorbiarn** Torbjörn.

It is characteristic that Rök, the longest inscription we know, is written in the main with short-twig runes. It may add interest to pay attention to the external form of the stone and the way in which the carver has covered the surface with runes. Inspection of the stone has led several scholars to think of rune-inscribed wooden tablets, and it is indeed possible to feel that the Rök stone represents a gigantic magnification of a wooden board with its surfaces tight-packed with runic characters.

Among other inscriptions that appear to imitate inscriptions on wood the one at Oklunda deserves mention. It is of quite a different type from the Rök inscription which essentially belongs to the memorial group. The Oklunda inscription is a *legal document* from pre-Christian times, cut in a little rock eminence by the farm Oklunda in Ö. Husby parish (Östergötland). It says, among other things, that the man who cut the runes had fled because of an offence—probably a killing—and to save his life had taken refuge in a holy place, the sanctuary at Oklunda. The begining of the inscription where this extremely interesting message is conveyed reads: **kunar : faþirunarþisaʀ : insa flausakaʀ : sutiuiþita** *Gunnarr faði runaʀ þessaʀ. En sa flo sakʀ. Sotti vi þetta...* "Gunnar cut these runes. And he fled under penalty. Sought this sanctuary..."

This is the earliest Scandinavian evidence we have of the right of asylum at a heathen cult-site. In the sanctuary Gunnar found an inviolable refuge, where no vengeance could touch him. The latter part of the inscription says that he made a settlement in accordance with law.

In connection with the Oklunda inscription it may be mentioned that an archaic prescription for atonement payments is found on the Forsa ring (Hälsingland), also cut in short-twig runes. A recent runological and linguistic investigation suggests that in all probability it is to be dated to the late ninth or early tenth century. Inscriptions of similar kind were doubtless made in considerable numbers, but of course almost exclusively on wood, the natural material for runic writing.

37

VIKING EXPEDITIONS IN THE LIGHT OF RUNIC INSCRIPTIONS

The great forays are generally felt to be the most typical expression of the Viking Age and the one that most catches the imagination. It is not inappropriate to give a more detailed account of what the rune stones can tell us of the Viking expeditions, for it was often precisely to commemorate kinsmen who had fallen in foreign lands that the stones were raised. When the great expeditions were over, the old trade routes closed, and the Viking ships no longer made ready each spring for voyages to east and west, then that meant the end of the carving and setting up of rune stones in the proper sense of the term. They may be called the monuments of the Viking voyages, and the sensitive reader may catch in many of their inscriptions the Viking's love of adventure and exploits of boisterous daring.

It should perhaps be emphasised that the Viking forays did not merely mean ferocious raids—they were also of great importance as a realisation of commercial policy. In the Viking Age the Norsemen were the chief middlemen in the commercial traffic between the Orient and western Europe. For long periods the Scandinavian North was at the focal point of world trade—a fact which is at once evident from the enormous finds of English and Arabic coins in Swedish soil.

As has often been observed, Swedish preoccupations in the Viking Age lay to the east, those of the Danes and Norwegians to the west. That is why Sweden is so seldom mentioned in the historical sources of western Europe, which do on the other hand—and naturally enough—offer plenty of reliable information about the western expeditions. East European sources provide material which is both scantier and more problematic; their relative sparseness makes the evidence of the rune stones all the more precious.

That Viking forays were not confined to west and east is shown straightway by a rune stone which makes part of the grand monument at Västra Strö (Skåne). There it says that a man called Fader "had these runes cut in memory of Assur, his brother, who met death *in the north on a Viking venture*" (*es norðr varð dauðr i vikingu*).

On the eastern route

The expeditions eastward had the longest tradition behind them. When the Viking Age began, the long waterways east and south of the Baltic were, it can be said, already functioning as the channels by which Swedish commerce with Byzantine and Arabian realms was maintained. They were the foundation of Sweden's position as a commercial power.

The oldest inscription to speak of a Viking expedition to the east is on the

Kälvesten stone (Östergötland), which can be dated to the ninth century: **stikuʀ
karþi kubl þau aft auint sunu sin ı sa fial austr miʀ aiuisli ı uikikʀ faþi aukrimulfʀ**

"Stygg (?) made these monuments in memory of Öjvind, his son. He fell in the east with Ejvisl. Viking cut and Grimulv."

The final sequence, **aukrimulfʀ**, must certainly be read as **auk krimulfʀ**. The final **k** in conj. **auk** must thus be read double (cf. p. 17 above: **is [s]laginaʀ**).

In **aukrimulfʀ** an attempt has been made to find an otherwise unknown personal name **riiulfʀ**. But the third rune is certainly **m**, slightly damaged at the top. The inscription is in short-twig runes, where **m** has the form †. This was easy to cut in wood but less so in hard, coarse granite: pieces readily flaked off when the short cross-stroke was cut through the top of the stave.

This stone from Västra Strö in Skåne was carved in memory of a man who went on a Viking foray not to east or west but north.

The oldest inscription that tells of a Viking expedition to the east is the one on the Kälvesten stone from Östergötland.

As we see, the stone was carved by two men, one called *Grimulfʀ*—a well-known name in the Viking Age, spread over the whole of Scandinavia, the other called *Vikingʀ*. It is interesting to find this name inscribed as early as the ninth century. It occurs on ten or so other Swedish stones but all a good deal younger than the Kälvesten instance. The name was common in medieval Norway.—The name of the dead man, *Øyvindr*, is found fairly frequently in Swedish inscriptions, but the Viking leader, *Æivisl*, has a name reliably attested only once elsewhere, on the famous Sparlösa stone (p. 31 above). Since the two rune stones appear to have been carved at about the same time and belong to districts closely connected in cultural terms, it is undeniably tempting to assume that both inscriptions refer to the same man. If that association is correct, then the Sparlösa stone was set up

Facing an old track which winds through an Uppland forest, the two Ed inscriptions tell us about a man who had been to Greece as "leader of the host" and who had this monument made in memory of his mother.

in memory of the man Öjvind had followed on the eastern route. Unfortunately, however, the Sparlösa inscription, partly because of damage in several places, contains some important cruces which are either uninterpreted or interpreted very doubtfully. We can never be absolutely confident that it is a monument to the memory of a battle-slain chieftain, despite the fact that among the pictorial elements on the stone we see a ship with birds hovering round the rigging. As things stand, the identification of Ejvisl on the two stones as the same man must remain no more than a possibility.

It is on the Kälvesten stone, then, that we meet the first certain example of a Swedish Viking leader who sailed to the east. Many followed in his wake. It is a pity that the inscription gives no precise information about the place where this evidently unsuccessful expedition met its fate. The same regrettable brevity is typical of most of our rune stones.

Unlike the first two centuries of the Viking Age, the eleventh century offers an almost overwhelming quantity of runic material. Many aspects of life in this period—one of rare vitality and variety in our history—are illuminated in quick flashes from the inscriptions. This is not least true of the eastward expeditions. The words which end the inscription on the Smula stone (Västergötland) could then have been said of many young men: *En þæiʀ urðu dauðiʀ i liði austr*, "they met death in the 'host' in the east".

The foreign country whose name occurs most frequently is Greece, *Grikkland*, denoting the northeast Mediterranean lands of the Eastern Empire. It is clear that journeys there were especially common, and to judge by the inscriptions it was a destination found particularly enticing by men from the central Swedish provinces. We must bear in mind, however, that conclusions of this kind are hazardous, since these provinces are so incomparably rich in rune stones.

It is not of course to be expected that the brief runic texts should give any detailed account of adventures met with on the expeditions, but a number of them at least tell us something more than the bare fact that the man in whose memory the stone was set up *varð dauðr i Grikkium*—"met death among the Greeks".

On a huge boulder at Ed, just north of Stockholm, are found two handsome inscriptions. They face an ancient track which winds through the forest along the shore of Edsjön. The inscriptions say:

·rahnualtr·lit·rista·runar·efʀ·fastui·moþur·sina·onems·totʀ·to i·
aiþi·kuþ·hialbi·ant·hena·
   runa·risti·lit·rahnualtr·huar a·griklanti·uas·lis·forunki·

"Ragnvald had the runes cut in memory of Fastvi, his mother, Onäm's daughter. She died in Ed. God help her soul.

<blockquote>
Ragnvald let
the runes be cut.
He was in Greece,
was leader of the host."
</blockquote>

This Ragnvald, whose name alone is enough to show he was of high birth, had thus by his own account been commander of a troop of warriors in Greece—*var a Grikklandi, vas liðs forungi*. All things considered, it seems most likely that the reference here is to that famous band of Norse mercenary soldiers, known as the Varangians, who were in the service of the Byzantine emperors at this time. One can readily appreciate Ragnvald's eagerness to announce to his contemporaries—

and to posterity—that he had held the distinguished post of commander in the Varangian corps in "Micklegard"—Constantinople. This élite corps in the imperial lifeguard, formed at the end of the tenth century, soon became famous. It was certainly a well-known institution to those who took the road past the boulder at Ed. To many a young man it breathed irresistible temptation to adventure.

That the voyages to Greece were frequent and on a large scale is also clearly indicated by one of our medieval provincial law-codes, which still retains a special provision concerning men who were in Greece. In the inheritance laws it says: "He takes no inheritance as long as he stays in Greece."

In the period when the Swedish Greek-stones were inscribed, there were livelier connections between Scandinavia and Byzantium than at any other time. Swedish Viking ships were then a common sight in the Black Sea, the Sea of Marmara, and the Ægean. And wider Mediterranean waters were sheared by their long keels.

The inscription at Ed contains the oldest record we have of the parish name Ed: Ragnvald's mother, Fastvi Onäm's daughter, died i · aiþi. *Æið* n. (ON *eið*, OSw. *eþ*) means "a neck of land between two stretches of water, over which vessels can be dragged". The "neck" which has given the parish its name appears to be the one in the northwest corner of Edsjön which interrupts direct communication with the extensive channels that lead to Sigtuna and Uppsala. (On place-names on rune stones see pp. 95 ff below.)

From Ragnvald's inscription we learn that he came home to Ed. He himself could tell of the honour he had won in Byzantium. But most of the runic inscriptions are memorials to men who sailed away and never returned. "They met death among the Greeks."

At Ulunda ford (west Uppland) stand two rune stones, one on either side of the spot where the road crosses the stream. Like the boulder at Ed these stones thus stand by a road—and a much more important road than the bridle-path by Edsjön. The ford at Ulunda is on *Eriksgata*, the road, that is, by which a newly elected king had to travel through the country to be acknowledged as ruler by the judgment of the people at their provincial assemblies. It is noteworthy how many rune stones were set up in the vicinity of this road, the most important highway in Sweden. (On rune stones erected *nær brautu* "near the road", see pp. 139 f below.)

The inscription on one of the Ulunda stones, raised by Kår and Kabbe, ends with a verse; the heir honours the dead man in these words:

For hæfila,	"He went boldly,
*fea*ʀ *aflaði*	wealth he won,
ut i Grikkium	out in Greece
arfa sinum.	for his heir."

Two rune stones in Södermanland also suggest the profits to be made on the Greek excursions. The one at Rycksta ends with the words: *For Olæifʀ i Grikkium, gulli skifti*; and in a verse couplet on one of the Grinda stones we find the same alliterative expression: *Vaʀ hann i Grikkium / gulli skifti* —"He was in Greece, took his share of gold".

Two rune stones stand on either side of Ulunda ford in Uppland, which was on the Eriksgata, the road by which a newly elected king had to travel through the country to be acknowledged as ruler in all the provinces.

One of the many Swedish runic monuments concerning men who journeyed to Greece is now preserved in England. What happened was that in the seventeenth century the English emissary in Stockholm sought permission on his royal master's behalf to export two Swedish rune stones to Oxford. Permission was granted by King Karl XI in 1687, and both stones joined the University's antiquarian collection. One of them is a typical Greek-stone, with the inscription:

ˈ þorstin ˈ lit×kera ˈ merki ˈ ftiʀ ˈ suin ˈ faþur ˈ sin ˈ uk ˈ ftiʀ ˈ þori ˈ broþur ˈ sin ˈ þiʀ ˈ huaru ˈ hut ˈ til ˈ k[ir]ika ˈ uk ˈ iftir ˈ inkiþuru ˈ moþur ˈ sin ˈ ybiʀ risti ˈ

Þorstæinn let gæra mærki æftiʀ Svæin, faður sinn, ok æftiʀ Þori, broður sinn. Þæiʀ vaʀu ut til Grikkia. Ok æftiʀ Ingiþoru, moður sin{a}. Øpiʀ risti.

This rune stone was raised at Ulunda ford by Kår and Kabbe.

45

"Torsten had the memorial made in memory of Sven, his father, and of Tore, his brother. They were abroad to Greece. And in memory of Ingetora, his mother. Öpir carved."

The father had evidently taken one of his two sons with him on the expedition to Greece. Torsten doubtless had to stay at home to look after the farm with Ingetora, his mother. The family lived in Ed, where the rune stone originally stood—not far from the boulder by Edsjön described above. Sven and Tore and Torsten must often have read the inscription that told of Ragnvald's successful journey to Micklegard and his career with the Varangians. Their expedition did not go so well. As the inscription shows, both father and son died out there.

The inscription is signed by Öpir, incomparably the most prolific of the rune-masters: we know over 80 inscriptions by him. He was an artist of rank, active in the last decades of the eleventh century, chiefly in the south and west of Uppland. His name was originally a nickname, nomen agentis (with suffix -*ia*-) to the verb *øpa* "shout, cry" (cognate with Engl. "weep"), so Öpir properly means "the bawler". As we learn from the signature on a couple of his stones, his true name was *Ofæigʀ*.

On the Ed stone we can observe some confusion on his part over the *h*-sound —he writes **hut** for **ut**. It is a dialect feature still well known in Roslagen, the eastern coastal part of Uppland. A good many Uppland inscriptions also show omission of initial *h*- (e.g. **an** for **han**, **agua · eli** for **hagua · heli** "cut the rock").

The voyagers to Greece steered their ships east across the Baltic. By the great river-systems of *Garðaríki* (Russia) they made their way "to Greek harbours", as it says on the stone at Fjuckby (Uppland) that Ljut the ship's captain set up in memory of one of his sons: ... *styrði knærri, kvam hann Grikkhafniʀ*... "He steered the ship, he came to Greek harbours".

There were several routes to choose from. Once the open waters of the Gulf of Finland were crossed, the ship could be brought by the channels of the river Neva in to Ladoga, where the trade-routes divided, one going in a southerly and one in an easterly direction. The usual route went by the river Volchov down to Old Ladoga, called *Aldeigjuborg,* or *Aldeigja*, by the Norsemen. (The name is undoubtedly a corruption of Ladoga; *Aldeigjuborg* thus means "Ladoga's burg".) Then the travellers had arrived in that vast territory which medieval Icelandic sources call *Svíþióð hin mikla*—"great Sweden" (*Scythia magna*). Archaeological investigations have shown that the Swedes had an important trading-post at Aldeigjuborg from the beginning of the ninth until towards the middle of the eleventh century. In 1950 a little runic inscription came to light there, cut on a piece of wood (fir). As one would expect, the runes are of the short-twig kind. The piece is probably from the ninth century and appears to contain two lines of verse. It is a find of great cultural and literary interest, and one which offers

This boulder at Esta in Södermanland is now badly damaged by weathering, but the text can be restored with the help of this drawing from the seventeenth century.

clear, written evidence of the penetration of Swedish culture in the Ladoga area very early in the Viking Age.

From Aldeigjuborg it was no great distance to the important commercial junction called *Holmgarðr,* Holmgård—Novgorod. It comes as no surprise to find this great station on the eastern route mentioned in the runic inscriptions of the homeland.

On a boulder at Esta (Södermanland) there is the following inscription, with its suggestion of strife in Holmgård: "Ingefast had the stone cut in memory of Sigvid, his father. He fell in Holmgård, the ship's captain, with his crew." (Unfortunately the Esta block is now badly damaged by weathering, but fortunately the text can be authentically restored with the help of a seventeenth-century drawing.) As in so many other instances, the last part of the inscription is in verse:

han fial	*Hann fiall*
i hulmkarþi	*i Holmgarði,*
skaiþaʀ uisi	*skæiðaʀ visi,*
miþ skibara	*með skipara.*

47

We see that on his voyage to Holmgård Sigvid had been *skæiðaʀ visi*—an interesting phrase with a poetic ring. (Syntactically it is, of course, in postpositional apposition to *Hann*.)

The word *skæið* f. "longship, warship (of larger dimensions)" is frequent in scaldic verse and West Norse prose literature. The Danish Tryggevælde inscription also contains the word—indeed, in its oldest occurrence since that stone was carved at the beginning of the tenth century. But its context on the Danish stone

On a boulder at Sjusta in Uppland it can be read that Runa had the famous rune carver Öpir make this memorial to Spiallbude, her husband, who met death in Holmgård (in Russia) in St Olav's church.

is surprising, for the introductory sentence of the inscription says that Ragnhild, Ulv's sister, had set up the stone and made the mound **auk skaiþ · þaisi** (*ok skæið þessi* "and this ship"). Here *skæið* must certainly be used of a "ship-setting", a series of stones set up to make the outline of a ship's hull, which Ragnvald had commissioned as a memorial to the dead man. With its deck of green turf and the gentle curve of the stone gunwale, rising in height at stem and stern, the ship-setting's affinity to the *skæið* is clear. The same word is used of the ships of the Varangians in the so-called Nestor Chronicle, the medieval Russian source which gives us important information about Swedish ventures to the east in the Viking Age. And to the west we find that the Anglo-Saxons borrowed the same word from the Norsemen (OE *scægð*).

For that matter, it was on a *skæið*—so *Ynglinga saga* tells us—that Haki, king of the Swedes, set sail with the ship itself as his funeral pyre. In his valiant fight on the Fyris fields he got such great wounds that his days, he knew, were numbered: *þá lét hann taka skeið er hann átti ok lét hlaða dauðum mǫnnum ok vápnum, lét þá flytia út til hafs ok leggia stýri í lag ok draga upp segl, en leggia eld í tyrvið ok gera bál á skipinu. Veðr stóð af landi. Haki var þá at kominn dauða eða dauðr, er hann var lagiðr á bálit. Sigldi skipit síðan logandi út í haf, ok var þetta allfrægt lengi síðan.* "Then he had a *skeið* fetched, one of his, and had it laden with dead men and weapons, had it moved out to open sea and the steering-oar shipped and the sail hoisted, and set fire to kindling and made a pyre on the ship. There was an offshore breeze. Haki was close to death or dead when he was laid on the pyre. Then the ship sailed blazing out to sea, and the fame of this lived long afterwards."

Like *skæið*, the word *visi* m. "leader, prince" is also well known from West Norse poetry. We find it several time in the *Edda*, e.g. in *Helgakviða Hundingsbana* I, v. 10:

> *Skamt lét vísi*   "The prince let battle
> *vígs at bíða.*   wait but briefly."

The word is a substantivisation of the adj. *viss* and so properly means "the wise one", but in an expression like *skæiðar visi* it was most probably associated with the verb *visa*, in the sense of "direct, lead".

Two bits of a rune stone have been found at Hallfrede in Follingbo parish (Gotland) which show that the stone was originally put up to commemorate a man who *do i Holmgarði* "died in Holmgård". The inscription throws light on something we learn from different, later sources—that the Gotlanders had a trading-post in Novgorod.

Another inscription of interest in this connection is found at Sjusta in Skokloster parish (Uppland). Two women, Runa and Sigrid, commissioned the rune-master Öpir (p. 46 above) to make an inscription in memory of four men, Spjallbude, Sven, Andvätt and Ragnar. These four were sons of Runa, a widow;

Sigrid is her daughter-in-law, once wife of Spjallbude and now widowed herself. Of him the inscription says: "He met death in Holmgård in Olav's church"—**an uar ˈ tauþr ˈ i hulmkarþi ˈ i olafs kriki** *Hann var dauðr i Holmgarði i Olafs kirkiu.* There can be little doubt but that by **kriki** Öpir meant *kirkiu,* dat. of the loanword *kirkia.* He often leaves out runes at the ends of words.

When we recall King Olav Haraldsson's personal connections with Holmgård, it is not particularly surprising that a church dedicated to this martyr-king should exist there as early as the latter part of the eleventh century. The inscription shows that this church was built in Novgorod in honour of his sanctity only a few decades after his death at Stiklestad in 1030. It also throws a

The piont called Domesnäs projects into the Gulf of Riga, a hazardous place to pass on one's way to Semgallen. Sven in memory of whom this stone at Mervalla was raised often sailed to Semgallen on his ship, a "knarr".

revealing light on another aspect of the Viking Age: the death toll was devastating.

The way by Ladoga, Aldeigjuborg, and Holmgård was the northernmost of the great routes to the east. A more southerly route had still older traditions. Rounding Domesnäs, the northern tip of Kurland, the ships sailed southeast across the Gulf of Riga towards the broad estuary of the Dvina, on whose calm lower reaches the voyage continued through the plains of Semgallen. Here, in Latvia, the existence of large Swedish colonies has been demonstrated by the archaeologist.

Both Domesnäs and Semgallen are named on the Mervalla stone (Södermanland), put up by Sigrid in memory of Sven, her husband. The memorial

This rune stone from Frugården in Västergötland recalls an ill-starred voyage: Sven was killed in Estonia.

inscription reads: **hn · uft · siklt · til · simkala · turum knari · um · tumisnis**

Hann oft siglt	"He often sailed
til Sæimgalla	to Semgallen
dyrum knærri	in dear-prized 'knarr'
um Domisnæs.	round Domesnäs."

Knarr (ON *knǫrr*) was the Norseman's name for his roomy sea-going ship, heavier and stronger than the longship. (It is indicative of the importance of Norse shipbuilding and seafaring that the word *knarr* was borrowed into so many languages: OE *cnearr*, Irish *cnarr*, Old French *canar*, OHG *gnarren*. The name may well have arisen from the creaking of the massive hull in the waves—cf. the verb *knarra* "creak" and the cognate (obsolete) English verb, "gnar(1)" = snarl, growl.) It was the *knarr* that carried the Norsemen over the great and perilous seas to Iceland and Greenland and Vinland the Good. No ocean was too vast for their vessels. The ships were the pride of the Norsemen, their great technical achievement, and it is natural that they should often be pictured by the artists of the time, sung of by scalds, and named in inscriptions commemorating the men who sailed them.

If a man had held command in a ship or was an owner, alone or in partnership, it was understandably seen fit to mention the fact in a runic epitaph. One of the stones in the great Västra Strö monument, for example, was put up by a co-owner in memory of "Björn, who owned a ship along with him".

It is worth noting that the phrase *dyrum knærri* (instrumental dat.) on the Mervalla stone has its exact verbal parallel in a well-known verse by Egill Skallagrímsson, composed in 920 according to the chronology of *Egils saga*. The young poet expresses his yearning for a ship and adventure; he wants to be off with Vikings—

> *standa upp í stafni,*
> *stýra dýrum knerri—*

"stand up in the stem, / steer the dear-prized *knarr*".

Domesnäs projects into the Gulf of Riga towards Runö and Ösel, and continues as a reef which gives no safe depth for some miles off the point. It is a treacherous place, hazardous for "dear-prized ships".

Semgallen is Latvian *Zemgale*, which is thought to mean "the low land". The Norsemen thus borrowed the name from Latvian. The same thing happened in other cases—cf. Virland, for example, which in Estonian is *Virumaa*, and Aldeigja from Ladoga (p. 47 above).

Virland comprises the northeast part of Estonia and so lies on the southern shores of the Gulf of Finland. Two men from Uppland fell there, Anund Kåresson and Björn Kättilmundsson. Anund, from the parish of Roslags-Bro,

Many rune stones in Gotland have the same shape as the picture stones. This Sjonhem stone was raised in memory of a man who lost his life at the river Venta on the Baltic shore.

uas · tribin + a + uirlanti—*vas drepinn a Virlandi* "was killed in Virland". Björn has two handsome runes stones to commemorate him, one of them in the great grave-field at Lunda:

rahnfriþ ı lit rasa stain þino ı aftiʀ biurn ı sun þaiʀa ı kitilmuntaʀ ı kuþ mialbi hons ant aukuþs muþiʀ hon fil a uirlanti ı in osmuntr markaþi. "Ragnfrid had this stone raised in memory of Björn, Kättilmund's son and hers. God and God's mother help his soul. He fell in Virland. And Åsmund cut."

The inscription is thus signed by Asmundr Karason, one of the great pioneers among rune-masters. He carved over 40 stones in Uppland and Gästrikland, half of them with his signature included. Most of them were probably inscribed in the 1020s and '30s but he seems to have been active much longer. His inscriptions have numerous characteristic features, some of them decidedly old-fashioned. He follows old tradition, for example, in letting a single rune serve as the last letter of one word and the first of the next. He also uses the ᚠ-rune for nasalised *a*. (Only a couple of decades later we find this rune used almost exclusively to denote *o*.) He uses division marks sparingly and dotted runes not at all (on the latter see pp. 29 f above).—It has been suggested that Asmundr Karason was an English cleric, referred to by Adam of Bremen as Osmundus, who later (about 1050) acted as archbishop under King Emund the Old. It is an identification which prompts interest but not belief.

Personal names such as *Æistfari* ("Estonia-farer"), *Æistulfʀ* and *Æistr*, which appear in runic inscriptions, testify at once to close connections with Estonia. (In all probability *Æistr* was originally a name for a slave of Estonian provenance.) Direct evidence of an ill-starred voyage to Estonia is also preserved on a rune stone at Frugården in Norra Åsarp parish (Västergötland):

kufi : rsþi : stin : þesi : eftʀ : ulaf : sun : sin · trk · hrþa · kuþan · hn · uarþ · trbin · i · estlatum · ... *Gufi ræisti stæin þennsi æftiʀ Olaf, sun sinn, dræng harða goðan. Hann varð drepinn i Æistlandum . . .*

"Guve raised this stone in memory of Olav, his son, a very noble 'dræng'. He was killed in Estonia..."

Southwest of Domesnäs lies *Windau* (Latvian *Ventspils*, Russian *Vindava*), one of the few harbours on this flat and unsheltered Baltic shore. It is the nearest haven for any ship sailing eastward from Gotland, and it was certainly often visited by traders from there. One of the fine stones in picture-stone form of the Sjonhem monument on Gotland was probably raised in memory of a man who

"Djärv got these scales from a man from Samland (or Semgallen)" is written on this little box found in Sigtuna.

lost his life at the mouth of the river Venta (Windau): **han : uarþ : tauþr : a : uitau :** *Hann varð dauðr a Vindфy.* The place-name *Winda* was taken by Norsemen to be *Vindфy,* "wind-isle", a natural enough folk-etymology in view of Swedish place-names like *Vindö* and *Väderö* ("wind-", "weather-").

Livonia, the country between Semgallen and Estonia, is also mentioned in two Swedish inscriptions of the Viking Age. On one of them, cut in the rock-face at Åda (Södermanland), we read:

: hermoþr : lit : hagua : at : barkuiþ : bruþur : sin : han trukn-þi : a lf : lanti : "Härmod had [the rock] cut in memory of Bergvid, his brother. He drowned in Livland."

A runic inscription of a different kind deserves notice at this point. It is engraved on a copper box discovered in Sigtuna. In the box a little pair of scales was kept, used for weighing gold and silver. Well over a hundred such scales have been found in the graves at Birka, Sigtuna's predecessor as the emporium of central Sweden: they were the insignia of the merchant.

The owner of the Sigtuna scales had his name inscribed on the box, and he also tells us how they came into his possession. The beginning of the inscription is of most interest to us at this point:

tiarfr×fik af×simskum×mạ**ni×skalaʀ×þisaʀ... in uirmuntr×faþi×runạr þisar** *Diarf*ʀ *fæk af sæmskum manni skala*ʀ *þessa*ʀ *... En Værmundr faði runa*ʀ *þessar*

"Djärv got these scales from a man from Samland (or Semgallen)... And Värmund incised these runes."

ON *skál* f., OSw. *skal, vægskal* f., means "the pan of a balance"; cf. Sw. *skålpund* "a pound as measured on weighing scales". In a medieval text (*Speculum Virginum*) we find, for instance, *rætuisonna skaal* "scales of justice". The pl. *skálar* on the Sigtuna box refers to the two pans, hence the weighing scales as a whole (cf. the pl. normal in English too).

The inscription, which is from the beginning of the eleventh century, does not give us altogether precise information about the provenance of Djärv's scales. The adj. *sæmskʀ* remains ambiguous: *af sæmskum manni* may mean that the man came from Samland but it may possibly mean from Semgallen. Semgallen, famous already in the time of the Elder Pliny as a source of the amber so highly prized in Rome, lies in East Prussia, in the southeast corner of the Baltic. (See further on the inscription p. 133 below.)

Before leaving these frequently visited Baltic coastlands, I may speak briefly of one or two inscriptions that tell of men who fell in Finland.

The inscription on a rune stone that once stood in Söderby-Karl parish in Roslagen (Uppland) and is now unfortunately lost said that "Björn and Igulfrid raised the stone in memory of Otrygg, their son. He was killed in Finland"—*a Finnlandi.* This inscription, which can be dated to the beginning of the eleventh century, is the oldest Swedish source in which the name of Sweden's eastern neighbour occurs. It is in itself natural that the name should be found on a stone in the coastal district of Roslagen in eastern Uppland, where many voyages to Finland had—and still have—their beginning. It must however be remembered that the name *Finnland* in Runic Swedish did not have the same significance as it has now. The area to which the name was then applied was certainly only that part which later, typically enough, was to be called Finland Proper, i.e. the southwestern part of the modern country. This coastal area, which is closer to Roslagen than any other part of the Finnish mainland, has thus in time given its name to the whole land. Here we may compare the similar development of the Finnish name for Sweden—*Ruotsi*. Originally this name was probably only used of Roslagen, the Uppland coastal region, but in time it became the Finnish name for the whole Swedish territory westward over the Baltic. When the rune stone commemorating Otrygg was inscribed, Swedish had no collective term for the different parts of Finland.

It was in a remoter Finnish province, in Tavastland, that a man named Egil lost his life. His stone at Söderby (Gästrikland) tells: *hann varð dauðr a Tafæistalandi.* He had taken part in a Viking expedition under the chieftain Fröger. Bruse, Egil's brother, had the splendid stone put up to his memory. Åsmund Kåresson and Sven cut the runes. Connections with Tavastland are also attested by the occurrence of the personal name *Tafæistr* in Runic Swedish.

As we just saw, the first time we meet the name of Finland is on the Söderby-Karl stone. A handsome grave-slab from Rute churchyard on Gotland offers a later example. It was placed over a man who "died in Finland".

We now leave these Baltic coastlands to follow the Swedes on their travels still farther to the east, guided by the terse directions of the runic memorials.

Immediately to the east of these coastal regions lay *Garðariki*, Gårdarike, where large commercial colonies were established along the ancient trade-routes. *Garðariki* most probably got its name from the many *garðar* "garths" (cf. Russian *gorod* "town") built to protect the trade-routes, in the same way as Castille in Spain is thought to have got its name from the *castella* put up by the Visigoths as a defence against the Moors. The commercial importance of Sweden in the Viking Age was based on the unique wealth of *Garðariki* in slaves, furs and hides. (Direct evidence of the Gotland fur-trade remains on the Stenkumla stone, erected in memory of a man who **sunarla : sat : miþ : skinum** *sunnarla sat með skinnum* "dealt in furs in the south".)

A profitable undertaking in *Garðariki* is clearly attested by the runic inscription on the Veda rock (Uppland): **þurtsain×kiarþif×tir irenmunt×sun sin aukaubti þinsa bu×auk×aflaþi×austr×i karþum** *Þorstæinn gærði æftiʀ Ærinmund, sun sinn, ok kaupti þennsa by ok aflaði austr i Garðum.*

"Torsten made it in memory of Ärnmund, his son, and bought this farm, and

made the money east in *Garðariki.*" The notice of the money made in Russia has alliteration and the movement of verse: *ok aflaði / austr i Garðum.*

The inscription also shows that inalienable land (*oðal*) could now be acquired by purchase. This must certainly have been the result of radical changes in society brought about by long-distance trading and Viking expeditions.

"East in *Garðariki*" is a familiar expression on Swedish rune stones. It occurs for example in the verse which ends the inscription on the Turinge stone (Södermanland): **bruþr uaʀu þaʀ bistra mana : a : lanti auk : i liþi : uti : hiltu sini huskarla : ui-+han+fial+i+urusti+austr+i+garþum+lis+furugi+lanmana+bestr**

Brøðr vaʀu þæiʀ	"The brothers were
bæstra manna	among the best men
a landi	on land
ok i liði uti,	and out in the host,

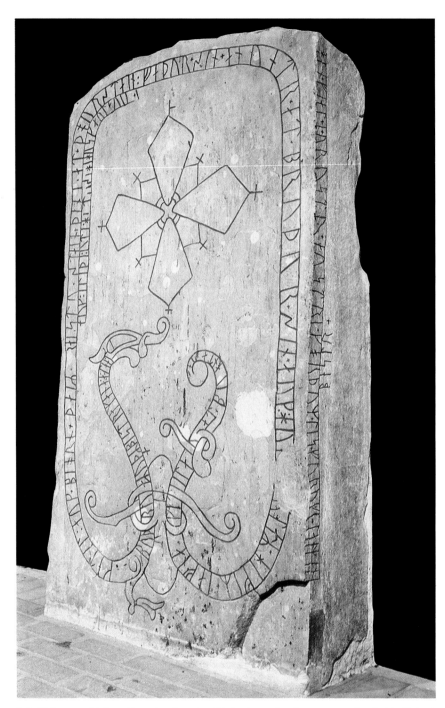

Left: This grave slab from Rute churchyard on Gotland was placed over a man who died in Finland. *Right:* On this stone in Turinge church in Södermanland family and retainers commemorate their chieftain Torsten and his brother.

heldu sina	treated their
huskarla vel.	retainers well.
Hann fiall i orrustu	He fell in action
austr i Garðum,	east in Garðariki,
liðs forungi,	the host's captain,
landmanna bæstr.	of 'land-men' the best."

This is the fine poem in which the Södermanland chieftain, Torsten, and his dead brother are commemorated by the surviving members of their family and their retainers.

At Gårdby church on Öland there is a rune stone which may claim some interest in this connection:

The Veda rock in Uppland was cut by a father in memory of his son an heir.

**harþruþr + raisti + stain + þinsa + aiftiʀ + sun + sin + smiþ + trak + kuþan +
halfburin + bruþiʀ ans + sitr × karþum brantr × riti + iak þu raþa khn**

"Härtrud set up this stone in memory of her son, Smed, a noble 'dræng'. Halvboren, his brother, stays in *Garðariki*. Brand cut [the runes] right so they can be read."

The expression **sitr×karþum** must obviously be interpreted as here, "stays, lives, in *Garðariki*" (cf. the sentence translated on p. 43 above, which renders the Inheritance Section 12:2 of *Äldre Västgötalagen*: *Ingsinss manss arv takær hæn mæn i girklandi sitær*).

It is true that it has been suggested that we should take the phrase to mean "stays in Gårdby", but this presupposes that the first element of Gårdby was the substantive *garðr*. This is not the case however: the first element is *gorr* (*går*), "dirt, muck". The name was originally *Gorby*; cf. the name of the neighbouring parish, *Sandby*.

The expeditions to Russia and through Russian territory are thus reflected again and again on the rune stones set up in the homefields of the voyagers, by the high road and at assembly places. And sometimes memorial runes were inscribed out on the distant routes themselves.

Near the mouth of the Dnieper, on the island Berezanj in the Black Sea, Grane buried his comrade, Karl. We know this from the gable-stone of a coffin discovered in excavations on Berezanj in 1905: **krani : kerþi : half : þisi : iftir : kal : fi : laka : sin** "Grane made this sarcophagus after Karl, his partner."

It appears from this that Karl and Grane were *félagaʀ,* partners who pooled their resources and undertook this trading venture together. The word *félagi* m. occurs in two other eleventh-century Swedish inscriptions.

Karl has his stone-coffin grave on an island whose sheltered bays have given protection to many a Swedish ship on the eastern voyage. When the traveller came from the north, with the perils of the Dnieper cataracts (mentioned on the Pilgård stone) and the difficulties of sandbanks and treacherous shoal-water still fresh in his memory, he came at last, here by Berezanj, to open water, where the Black Sea, bigger than the Baltic, opened up before his ship's prow. And when he came to Berezanj from the south—on his way home to the thick-wooded creeks of Mälaren or the stony havens of Gotland—he could gather strength here before being forced to bend back and oar in the long struggle against the river currents and all the other obstacles on his way. Soon enough the time would come for the unloading and the dragging over the portages and the reloading, all in the sticky heat of the interior, hardly relieved by the steppe winds and the summer rain. And all the while his longing for a sail-bellying breeze and salt water grew stronger.

At Gårdby church on Öland there is a rune stone which Härtrud had raised in memory of her son Smed.

Another Swedish inscription which it is natural to mention in company with the Berezanj slab is the one on the *Piræus lion*. This magnificent marble lion had kept guard in Porto Leone, the harbour of Athens, for many centuries before a Swedish Viking incised his inscription on its flanks. The serpent-band, filled with runes, coils itself round the classic marble in just the same way as on the Uppland granite. Unfortunately, the inscription is now for the most part illegible, for since it was cut the lion has suffered much from battles in the harbour as well as from wind and weather. (The victorious Venetians carried off the lion as a trophy in 1687 and it now stands in Venice—where its runes were finally recognised for what they are by a Swedish diplomat, the Egyptologist Johan David Åkerblad.)

In a region that lay between Berezanj and the Piræus—in Wallachia—the Gotlander Rodfos was treacherously killed by men beyond the reach of family vengeance. One of the handsome rune stones of the Sjonhem monument tells us of his fate:

roþuisl : auk : roþalf : þau : litu : raisa : staina : eftir : sy[ni : sina :] þria : þina : eftir : roþfos : han : siku : blakumen : i : utfaru kuþ : hielbin : sial : roþfoaʀ kuþ : suiki : þa : aʀ : han : suiu :

"Rodvisl and Rodälv, they had the stones set up in memory of their three sons. This one in memory of Rodfos. Wallachians betrayed him on an expedition. God help Rodfos's soul. God betray those who betrayed him."

As the name of a people, **blakumen** must clearly mean the inhabitants of Wallachia, the southernmost part of present-day Rumania. This region—in the Migration Age a playground for Vandals, Marcomanni, Gepids, Langobards and other tribes—was ruled in the eleventh century by the Turkish people called the Cumans. The **blaku** on the rune stone may be compared with Old Slavonic *vlachu*: in early Gotlandic the combination *vl-*, unknown in Old Scandinavian, was replaced by *bl-*. The second element is naturally *-mænn* "men". (In Swedish the word *valack* has long been used of a "gelding": its proper sense is "horse from Wallachia".)

We cannot say for certain what kind of expedition Rodfos was on when he was killed, but it seems most likely that it was a trading venture.

In the last sentence—*Guð sviki þa, eʀ hann sviku*—we find a formula typical of the transition from paganism to Christianity. The duty of vengeance on the inaccessible slayers of their son is handed over to God. There can as yet be no question of forgiving those who trespass against us.

The largest and from some points of view the most interesting group of stones commemorating the eastern expeditions comprises, however, the so-called Ingvar stones. They were put up in memory of men who had followed Ingvar the Far-travelled on his long journey to Serkland.

It is impossible to define the boundaries of the rune stones' *Serkland*—"the Saracens' land". The Norsemen probably meant by it the lands of the Abbasid caliphate, whose capital in the Viking Age was Baghdad.

Ingvar's expedition is mentioned on nearly thirty rune stones, most of them found in the Mälar region. It undoubtedly attracted many participants and must have been one of the great events in the central Swedish districts in the first half of the eleventh century. The inscriptions show clearly that this bold Viking venture met a dismal end. Not a single one refers to a man who returned from those far-off lands. All the members of the expedition died "south in Serkland". Through a hazy distance the rumour of the disaster filtered home to their native hamlets.

The rune stone at Lundby in Södermanland as it appears in Richard Dybeck's "Svenska Run-Urkunder", published in 1885, an illustration which mirrors the national romanticism of the age. The stone belongs to the so-called Ingvar group.

On a rune stone at Stora Lundby (Södermanland), for example, we read: : **sbiuti : halftan : þaiʀ : raisþu : stain : þansi : eftiʀ : skarþa : bruþur sin : fur : austr : hiþan : miþ : ikuari : ą sirklanti : likʀ : sunʀ iuintaʀ**

Spiuti, Halfdan, þæiʀ ræisþu stæin þannsi æftiʀ Skarða, broður sinn.

> *For austr heðan*
> *með Ingvari.*
> *A Særklandi liggʀ*
> *sunʀ Øyvindaʀ.*

"Spjute, Halvdan, they raised this stone in memory of Skarde, their brother.

> Went east from here
> with Ingvar.
> In Serkland lies
> the son of Öjvind."

Ingvar's expedition has its noblest monument in the inscription on the Gripsholm stone. It was set up by Tola in memory of her son, Harald. According to the runes, he was Ingvar the Far-travelled's brother:

✕tula : lit : raisa : stain : þinsat : sun : sin : haralt : bruþur : inkuars : þaiʀ furu : trikila : fiari : at : kuli : auk : a : ustarlar : ni : kafu : tuu : sunar : la : a sirk : lan : ti

Tola let ræisa stæin þennsa at sun sinn Harald, bróður Ingvars.

Þæiʀ foru drængila	"They fared like men
fiarri at gulli	far after gold
ok austarla	and in the east
ærni gafu.	gave the eagle food.
Dou sunnarla	They died southward
a Særklandi.	in Serkland."

It undeniably strikes one as rather peculiar that Tola raised a rune stone only in memory of her son Harald and referred only in passing, as it were, to his famous brother, Ingvar, the leader of the expedition, as a means of further identifying Harald and adding lustre to his name. Three possible explanations can be found for this, on the face of it, surprising mode of expression. Ingvar may have had a stone of his own, set up beside his brother's and since lost. It could have been used for building purposes in the same way as Harald's was. (The Gripsholm stone was discovered as a threshold flagstone in the bottom vault of the east tower of the castle there.) The second conceivable reason is that "brother" in the inscription does not have its usual family sense but refers to membership of the same fraternity: "foster-brother", "brother in arms", "sworn retainer"—such a sense is securely attested on the Hällestad stone in Skåne (see p. 86). The third possibility is that Ingvar was not Tola's son and was thus only a half-brother of Harald.

It is clear that Tola's husband, the father of the two brothers, was dead when the Gripsholm stone was inscribed—otherwise Tola would not have set it up solely on her own account. Who then was the father of Ingvar and Harald?

The fame of Ingvar spread far and wide. He is the hero of the Icelandic *Yngvars saga víðforla*, where his expedition is described in the fantastical manner of the so-called legendary sagas (*fornaldarsögur*). The saga, which was written a good 200 years and more after the end of the ill-fated expedition, says that Ingvar's father was named *Eymundr: Nú fór Eymundr ór Garðaríki með mikilli sæmd ok virðingu af allri alþýðu ok kemr nú til Svíþjóðar ok sezt at ríki sínu ok eignum, ok brátt aflar hann sér kvánfangs ok fær ríks manns dóttur, ok gat við henni einn son, er Yngvarr hét.* Eymund is thus said to have returned from Garðaríki to Sweden, where he married the daughter of a mighty man "and had with her a son, who was called Yngvar".

It is in fact possible that the saga's report of his father's name may be corroborated by the inscription on a rune stone at Strängnäs. Unfortunately, the stone is only fragmentarily preserved and this inevitably makes for some uncertainty about the association. The names of the dead men are not contained on what is left of the stone but their description as **suni : aimuntaʀ** "sons of Emund" remains. What makes the Ingvar association possible is the interesting fact that the formulation of the Strängnäs inscription clearly corresponded to that on the Gripsholm stone. On the stone remnant we find these fragmentary words, evidently from a verse, ... **sunarla : a : serkl** ... *sunnarla a Særklandi* "southward in Serkland". It would be a cause for celebration if the lost bits of the Strängnäs stone were one day restored to us.

In *Yngvars saga víðforla* (and in three of the Icelandic annal compilations) we are given the following date for the death of this high-born Viking leader: *En þá er Yngvarr andaðist, var liðit frá burð Jesú Kristi MXL ok einn vetr. Þá var hann hálfþrítugr, er hann dó. Þat var ellefu vetrum eftir fall Ólafs konungs ins helga Haraldssonar.* "And when Yngvar died, 1041 winters had passed since the birth of Jesus Christ. He was then twenty-five when he died. It was eleven winters after the fall of King Olav the Saint, son of Harald."

It should perhaps be mentioned that the phrase in the Gripsholm verse, "give the eagle food", means to "kill enemies". It is a well-known expression in eddaic and scaldic verse. Helge Hundingsbane, for example, interrupts a flyting between Sinfjötle and Gudmund with the words:

Væri ykr, Sinfjǫtli,	"More fitting, Sinfjötle,
sæmra miklu	by far for you both
gunni at heyja	to give now battle
ok glaða ǫrnu,	and gladden eagles
en sé ónýtum	than with useless words
orðum at bregðask . . .	upbraid each other."

The warriors slain by Erik Blood-axe, whose bodies are strewn over the battlefield at the end of the day, are called "the eagle's supper" by Egill Skallagrímsson (*náttverð ara*; *Hǫfuðlausn*, v. 10), and we find many similar pictures in scaldic verse. In the poetry of the Vikings eagle and raven hover over the carnage, thirsting for the blood of dead and wounded men; they sate their hunger on

Right: A ship's captain named Gunnlev knew well "how to steer a ship" but was "killed in the east with Ingvar". His memorial is an impressive rune stone at Varpsundet in Uppland. *Left:* This rune stone stands outside Gripsholm castle. It was put up in memory of Ingvar the Far-travelled's brother Harald.

the corpses. The wolf, "the horse of the witchwoman" (*flagðs goti, flagðs hestr*), roams there, scouting for food (cf. "the horse of the Valkyrie" on the Rök stone, p. 33 above). In the eddaic poem called *Guðrúnarkviða in forna* all these ravening beasts of the battle field come together in the stanza in which Högne pitilessly tells Gudrun of the death of Sigurd, her husband:

Líttu þar Sigurð	"See Sigurd there
á suðrvega!	on the southern ways!
Þá heyrir þú	Then you will hear
hrafna gialla,	ravens screaming,
ǫrnu gialla,	eagles screaming,
ætsli fegna,	joyous at food,
varga þióta	wolves howling
um veri þínum.	over your husband."

How many ships took part in Ingvar's expedition cannot be determined. Once or twice, it is true, captains are mentioned who joined him and steered their own ships, but of course we cannot expect the rune stones to give us a full tally of his fleet. On the Svinnegarn stone (Uppland), originally part of an imposing monument that probably stood on the assembly place at Svinnegarn, parents had this epitaph inscribed for their son:

þialfi×auk×hulmnlauk×litu×raisa×staina þisa×ala×at
baka×sun sin×is ati×ain×sir×skib×auk×austr×stu[rþi×]
i×ikuars×liþ×kuþ hialbi×ot×baka×askil×raist

Þialfi ok Holmlaug letu ræisa stæina þessa alla at Banka, sun sinn.
Es atti æinn sᴇʀ skip ok austr styrði i Ingvars lið. Guð hialpi and Banka.
Æskill ræist.

"Tjälve and Holmlög had all these stones set up in memory of Banke, their son. He had a ship of his own and steered eastward in Ingvar's host. God help Banke's soul. Äskil carved." (In *atti æinn sᴇʀ*, "alone owned for himself", *sᴇʀ* is the dat. of the third person reflexive pron.)

Of another Uppland man the Steninge inscription—clearly also the work of Äskil—says that "he steered a ship eastward with Ingvar"—*Es styrði austr skipi með Ingvari*... The Varpsund stone is also of interest, raised in memory of the ship's captain Gunnlev, who *vas austr með Ingvari drepinn*, "killed in the east with Ingvar". His memory lives in the terse but pregnant sentence: *Es kunni vel knærri styra*, "He well knew how to steer a ship".

The writer of *Yngvars saga* says that Yngvar had thirty ships in his fleet—probably something of an exaggeration. As a whole the saga must be characterised as a romantic fiction spun round a kernel of historical fact. If it were not for the positive and contemporary evidence of the rune stones, then the greatest of all Swedish enterprises in the Viking Age would, like so much else, have been lost to history.

On the Varpsund stone just mentioned we saw that the dead man was remembered with honour as one who "well knew how to steer a ship". In the age of the rune stones the commander of a vessel was called *styrimaðr*, "steersman,

Banke's parents had this stone raised at Svinnegarn in Uppland in memory of their son who "had a ship of his own and steered eastward in Ingvar's host".

This rune stone was found a few years ago during excavation and restoration of Uppsala Cathedral. It was originally set up to commemorate Vigmar who was a 'steersman', that is commander of a ship.

the man at the helm", and we meet several such in our Viking Age inscriptions. A stone found in almost perfect condition a few years ago was set up by three sons in memory of their father, Vigmar—**styriman · koþan**. The stone came to light in the course of excavation under a buttress in Uppsala Cathedral—a building notably rich in rune stones.

A very fine example of a "steersman stone" is the Örby stone from Rasbo parish, which now stands in Uppsala. It was inscribed and erected by Vigmund and Åfrid—the latter a rare woman among the rune-masters. It reads: **uihmuntr ı lit ı agua · stain · at ı sig ı selfon ı slyiastr ı mono ı guþ ı ialbi sial ı uihmuntar · styrimons uihmuntr · auk ı afiriþ : eku merki ı at kuikuan · sik** · *Vigmundr let haggva stæin at sik sialfan, slœgiastr manna. Gud hialpi sial Vigmundaʀ styrimanns. Vigmundr ok Afrid hioggu mærki at kvikvan sik.*

On a pilgrimage to Jerusalem Östen died in Greece. His wife and sons raised the memorial.

"Vigmund, shrewdest of men, had the stone cut in memory of himself. God help the soul of Vigmund the steersman. Vigmund and Åfrid cut the memorial in his lifetime."

In the company of two other rune stones from Uppland, the Örby stone had the honour of representing Sweden at the Universal Exhibition in Paris in 1867—where they won a bronze medal. The carriage to Paris went smoothly but the Örby stone had an adventurous time on the way back. During reloading at Le Havre, the handsome stone went overboard. Since the three stones were insured for a total of 600 Swedish kronor, the insurance company paid out kr 200 for the Örby stone. It lay at the bottom of the muddy harbour for thirty years but then, as luck would have it, the harbour had to be dredged. The dredge came upon the great heavy rune stone and scooped it up undamaged. It was then sent home to Uppsala and set up there once more. To the best of my knowledge, the insurance money was never repaid.

The courses and destinations of these captains, these steersmen, to what lands and havens their navigation took them, usually find no record in their concise epitaphs. An exception is the inscription on the Fjuckby stone (Uppland), set up by *Liutr styrimaðr* in memory of two sons. Of one of them it says that "he steered his ship to Greek harbours". We see that both Ljut and one of his sons were ship's captains.

It was not only to win gold and "feed eagles" that men voyaged eastward. Journeys were made to Jerusalem for other reasons.

At Broby bridge in Täby parish, just north of Stockholm, stand two rune stones raised in memory of Östen by his sons and his wife. One of the things the inscriptions tell us is that Östen went out to Jerusalem and died in Greece: ×is×suti×iursalir auk antaþis ubi×kirkum *Es sotti Iorsaliʀ ok ændaðis uppi i Grikkium.* His pilgrimage was probably made at about the same time as King Canute the Great went to Rome (1027), where he founded a hospice for pilgrims from Scandinavia.

Another pilgrimage, also undertaken in the first half of the eleventh century, is attested by the handsome inscription which Ingerun, Hård's daughter, had carved as her own memorial at Almarestäket, west of Stockholm.

It is thanks to that industrious "seeker of antiquities", Mårten Aschaneus, that we know what the Almarestäket rock and its inscription looked like, even though it had already disappeared by the end of the seventeenth century. He copied the inscription not many years after 1600 and described its situation in this way: "These pilgrim's runes are on a rock by Lilla Hiderstäk, north of the public bridge. West of Almarestäk. Towards the south." A few decades later Johan Peringskiöld added some details about the site: "The high road to Lilla Stäket goes round a steep slope, now called Dalekarlsbacken, on the rock-face of which there is a remarkable runic inscription cut in a shield-shape 2 ells high and 1 ½ ells wide, situated north of the public bridge and west of Almarestäk, with the inscription facing south, but now so completely covered with earth and brushwood by road-workers raising the road-level that it can no longer be seen—and therefore fortunate that we possess the copy which the late antiquarian, Hr Mårten Aschaneus of Bårgby, made with his pen from the rock itself fifty years ago..." According to Aschaneus, the inscription read:

· iskirun · harþiʀ · totiʀ · lit · risti · runiʀ · ati · sik · sialfan · hn · uil · austr · fara · auk · ut · til · iursala · fair · risti · runiʀ ·

Aschaneus undoubtedly misread the runes in a number of places. It is very probable that the following offers an accurate transliteration:

Ingirun, Harðaʀ dottiʀ, let rista runaʀ at sik sialfa. Hon vill austr fara ok ut til Iorsala. Fotr risti runaʀ.

"Ingerun, Hård's daughter, had the runes cut in memory of herself. She means to go east and out to Jerusalem. Fot cut the runes."

A rune stone found in Uppsala Cathedral refers to a man who "died in the south". Remarkably enough, the expression *vaʀ dauðr i suðr* occurs nowhere else in Swedish inscriptions. We cannot exclude the possibility that it meant that he died on a pilgrimage: cf. ON *suðrferð, -før, ganga suðr*—normal expressions with reference to pilgrimage to Rome.

Langbarðaland—Lombardy but used by Norsemen as a general term for Italy—was also reached by way of Greece. Gudlög put up two rune stones in memory of her son, Holme, who lived in Fittja in Täby parish (Uppland) but who died *a Langbarðalandi*:

kuþluk × lit · raisa · staina · at · hulma · sun · sin · han · to · a · lank · barþa · lanti×

And the runic epitaph of Olev which Inga, his mother, had inscribed on his stone at Djulefors (Södermanland) ends with this highly-wrought verse, with ringing alliteration and assonance:

: han : austarla :	*Hann austarla*
arþi : barþi :	*arði barði*
auk : o : lakbarþ[a]	*ok a Langbarða*
lanti : antaþis	*landi andaðis.*

"He to the eastward / ploughed with his prow / and in Langobard's / land met his end."

A rune stone, sadly much damaged, found at Lagnö in Vansö parish (Södermanland) is also of interest in this context. It says of the dead man: **: han : iʀ : entaþr : i : austruiki : ut : o : la-...** This fragment is probably to be read: *Hann eʀ ændaðr i austrvegi ut a Langbarðalandi.*

These men who died in Italy were probably Varangians in the service of the Byzantine emperor.

Archaeological discoveries put the rune stones' sketchy references to eastern voyages in a deeper perspective. Large hoards of Arabic coins and oriental jewellery have been dug up in Swedish soil. The commerce with *Garðariki*, Micklegard and the East brought great wealth to Sweden, and fostered contacts with the civilisation of Byzantium and the Orient. We are justified in seeing many of the voyages as part of a calculated and effective commercial policy, and as a whole it may be said that it was on the eastern routes that the Swedes made their most significant contribution to European history in the Viking Age.

In some cases the runic obituaries show that young men from the same family tried their luck in different directions. A rune stone from Dalum parish in Västergötland commemorates two brothers and ends: **eʀ : uarþ · tuþr uestr : en · anar : austr :** *Eʀ varð dauðr vestr, en annarr austr*—"One died in the west and the other in the east". And Gunnald put up two stones at Berga in Skultuna parish (Västmanland), one in memory of his son, Gerfast, *dræng goðan, ok vas farinn til Ænglands,* the other in memory of his stepson, Orm, *dræng goðan, ok vas farinn austr með Ingvari.*

We learn of other men who had made the eastward journey that they had also been on board when a different course was set. The Tystberga stone (Södermanland) was erected in memory of Holmsten who had first been "long in the west" but who had then returned and with one of his sons, Rodger, had sailed away with Ingvar—and with him "they died in the east". We discover this from the four lines of *fornyrðislag* which end the inscription:

han hafþi : ystarla	*Hann hafði vestarla*
um : uaʀit : lenki :	*um vaʀit længi.*
tuu : a : ustarla :	*Dou austarla*
meþ : inkuari	*með Ingvari.*

We need not doubt that **ystarla** is rightly read as *vestarla*—it is demanded by the alliteration on *v-*: *vestarla—vaʀit.* The second couplet has vowel alliteration: *austarla—Ingvari.*

These men who had been both "westward and eastward" had come into contact with two very different civilisations. It is not hard to imagine their wonderment at what they saw, these locals from Uppland, Södermanland and Småland. There can be little doubt but that at first they would feel more at home in the western Germanic world than in the Byzantine-Oriental atmosphere, with its gardens and oases, its desert regions quivering in the heat-haze, its richly decorated buildings and its inquisitive and motley multitudes. But in the west too they saw much that, at least to begin with, must have seemed incomprehensible and foreign. They encountered a highly developed western culture and made fruitful contact with a politically divided Europe. And if luck was on their side, whether they sailed east or west, they came home again with the fresh and influential knowledge that was part of their profit from having seen the world.

On the western route

The fact that the name England occurs nearly as often as that of Greece in the runic inscriptions of the early eleventh century is at once enough to show that westward voyages were also common. In several cases, however, the country or countries visited in the west are not defined by name. All that is said on the Kjula stone (Södermanland) of the dead chieftain Spjut, for example, is that "he had been in the west":

At Kjula ås in Södermanland this impressive rune stone was set up in memory of Spjut "who had been in the west".

Saʀ vestarla	"He in the west
um veʀit hafði,	had been,
borg um brutna	township taken
ok um barða.	and attacked."

And on the Spånga stone (Södermanland) Gudmar's memorial is worded like this: **stuþ : triki : la · i · stafn skibi : likʀ uistarla...**

Stoð drængila	"He stood like a man
i stafn skipi.	in the stem of the ship.
Liggʀ vestarla . . .	He lies in the west . . ."

The Härlingstorp stone (Västergötland) was put up in memory of a man of whom the inscription says: **sa × uarþ : tuþr : o : uastr : uakm : i : uikiku** *Sa varð dauðr a vestrvegum i vikingu* "He met death on the 'western routes' on a Viking venture."

To some extent the Viking forays to the west had a different character from the eastern voyages. In one respect at least, however, there is a striking external similarity: the Varangian Guard of the Eastern emperors had its parallel institution in the famous body of retainers of Canute the Great, the bodyguard called *þingalið*. Membership of this renowned corps of distinguished and well-trained warriors was an honour eagerly sought. Gere from Kålsta in Häggeby parish (Uppland) was a member and his sons did not omit to mention it in his epitaph: "Stärkar and Hjorvard had this stone set up in memory of their father Gere, who in the west had his place in the *þingalið* (*sum vestr sat i þingaliði*). God help his soul."

A rune stone from Landeryd (Östergötland) also deserves mention in this connection. It reads: · **uirikʀ : resti : stan : eftiʀ: þialfa : bruþur : sin : trak : þan : aʀ · uaʀ miʀ · knuti:** *Væringʀ ræisti stæin æftiʀ Þialfa, broður sinn, dræng þann, eʀ vaʀ meðr Knuti.* "Väring raised the stone in memory of Tjälve, his brother, the 'dræng' who served with Canute." It is of some interest to note that the man who set up the stone, the dead man's brother, is called Väring (= Varangian). In this way the Landeryd stone carries the reader's thoughts both to the Varangians of Micklegard and to the royal body guard of England.

The name London occurs on the Valleberga stone. (Skåne). It was erected in memory of two men, Manne and Svenne, who found their graves in London. The end of the inscription says: *Guð hialpi sial þæiʀa vel. En þæir liggia i Lundunum* "May God help their souls well. And they lie in London."

It may be mentioned that two stones with runes on them have been found in the heart of London itself, one of them in St Paul's churchyard. Both were parts of coffins from the first half of the eleventh century.

In a similar sort of stone coffin lies Gunnar, Rode's son, from Småland. He is buried in Bath. His brother buried him there; his son raised his runic monument at home in Nävelsjö in Småland: **: kuntkel : sati : sten : þansi : eftir : kunar : faþur : sin : sun : hruþa : halgi : lagþi : han : i : sten : þr : bruþur : sin : a : haglati : i : baþum** *Gunnkell satti stæin þennsi æftiʀ Gunnar, faður sinn, sun Hroða. Hælgi lagði hann i stæinþro, broður sinn, a Ænglandi i Baðum.* "Gunnkel placed this stone in memory of Gunnar, his father, Rode's son. Helge laid him, his brother, in a sarcophagus in England in Bath."

A Swedish rune stone from Schleswig tells of a man who "rests in England in 'Skia'"—a place so far unidentified.

Stones of especial historical interest are those which mention the Danegeld, the tribute payments that from the end of the tenth century onwards were imposed on the English people to buy off Viking attacks. The huge finds of English silver in Swedish soil give some idea of the size of these payments. There are more English silver coins from this period in Swedish museums than there are in England itself. At Betby in Österhaninge parish (Södermanland) there is a rune stone set up in memory of Järund: : aʀ · uaʀ : uestþr : meþ : ulfi : suni · hakunar · *Er var vestr með Ulfi, syni Hakonar* "He was in the west with Ulv, Håkon's son". And just by Betby, sunk in a river, a silver hoard has come to light which included a couple of hundred English coins minted in the Viking Age.

To this group belong the notable Yttergärde stones (Uppland), inscribed in the 1020s. They were set up by Karse and Karlbjörn in memory of their father, Ulv of Borresta, a great yeoman of Uppland. The inscription on one of the stones reads: **in ulfr hafir onklati · þru kialtakat þit uas fursta þis tusti kalt · þa [kalt] þurktil · þa kalt knutr** *En Ulfʀ hafiʀ a Ænglandi þry giald takit. Þet vas fyrsta þet's Tosti galt. Þa galt Þorkætill. Þa galt Knutr.* "And Ulv took in England three gelds. That was the first which Toste paid. Then Torkel paid. Then Canute paid."

This terse statement, with which the sons saw fit to commemorate their dead father, was full of meaning to their contemporaries. An adventurous career is traced here in phrases that could hardly be more laconic. Ulv's contemporaries

The Landeryd stone from Östergötland commemorates Tjälve who served in the royal bodyguard of England.

Gunnar from Nävelsjö in Småland died and was buried in Bath. At home his son raised a runic monument to his memory.

could not read this inscription without hearing the tempting chink of good English silver. And their ears must have been filled too with the familiar sound and surge of the North Sea waves.

Toste, who was the first to pay Ulv his share of the tribute money, was probably the Swedish Viking leader mentioned once or twice by Snorri Sturluson. In the *Heimskringla* he writes: *Tósti hét maðr í Svíþjóð, er einn var ríkastr ok gofgastr í því landi, þeira er eigi bæri tígnar-nafn. Hann var inn mesti hermaðr ok var longum í hernaði; hann var kallaðr Skoglar-Tósti.* "Toste was the name of a man in Sweden, one of the mightiest and most respected of men in that land who had no title of rank. He was a very great warrior and spent long periods on campaigns abroad. He was called Sköglar-Toste [= Toste of the Valkyrie,

The sons of the great yeoman Ulv of Borresta set up a stone in memory of their father. He took three gelds in England.

Battle-Toste]." According to Snorri, Toste was the father of the Sigrid who was called "the lady of great undertakings" (*in stórráða*), and in that case he had as sons-in-law two of the most renowned figures in this obscure period of Scandinavian history towards the end of the tenth century: the Swedish king, Erik the Victorious, and the Danish king, Sven Forkbeard.

The second leader who distributed payment to Ulv was Torkel the Tall, chief of the Jomsvikings and a figure swathed in legend. He was involved in more than one attack on England in the early years of the eleventh century.

The third was Canute, Sven Forkbeard's son. He became ruler of England at the beginning of 1017, and in 1018 he paid the last and biggest Danegeld to his homeward-bound Viking troops.

Toste, Torkel and Canute were the names of the leaders in whose wake Ulv of Borresta had sailed to England. They were names that indeed deserved record on Ulv's rune stone, names that added lustre to the mighty yeoman of Uppland and his family. And with the rune stone the sons thanked their father for the inheritance he had left them of wealth and honour.

Another Uppland man who "received Canute's payment" and came back to his farm safe and sound was Alle in Väsby. He saw to the preparation of his own monument, on which he records his proud exploit: *Alli let ræisa stæin þenna æftiʀ sik sialfan. Hann tok Knuts giald a Ænglandi. Guð hialpi hans and!* "Alle had this stone raised in memory of himself. He took Canute's geld in England. God help his soul."

One of the Lingsberg stones (Uppland) says among other things that Ulvrik had taken two payments in England (*Hann hafði a Ænglandi tu giald takit*). And on the Grinda stone, also from the first decades of the eleventh century, it says that Gudve was west in England and took his share of a Danegeld payment—*Guðveʀ vaʀ vestr a Ænglandi, gialdi skifti.* See pp. 89 f.

Many Swedes at that time might have had the same memorial as Hävner Torstensson (Bjudby, Södermanland):

Vaʀ til Ænglands	"To England had
ungʀ drængʀ farinn,	the young 'dræng' fared,
varð þa hæima	then at home
at harmi dauðr.	lamented died."

Canute the Great was not the only ruler of England to be named on Swedish rune stones. It is most likely that it is his son and successor, Harald Harefoot, who is referred to on the Tuna stone (Småland): *Tummi ræisti stæin þennsi æftiʀ Assur, broður sinn, þann eʀ vaʀ skipari Haralds konungs* "Tumme raised this stone in memory of Assur, his brother, who was King Harald's crew-man".

One of the two Sävsjö stones (Småland) commemorates a man who had held the important post of *stallare*, "marshal", under Håkon Jarl: **tufa : risti : stin : þina : eftir : ura : faþur : sin : stalara : hkunaʀ : iarls** "Tova raised this stone in memory of Vråe, her father, Håkon Jarl's marshal". We cannot be perfectly sure who this Håkon Jarl was, but it seems likely that he was Canute the Great's nephew and ally, a member of the famous dynasty of the Lade-jarls of Norway. Håkon was drowned in the Pentland Firth in 1029. Tova, daughter of his marshal from Småland, erects the stone in memory of her father, proudly conscious of the fact that he had once held one of the highest offices at Håkon Jarl's court. There were other English voyagers in her family too; we are told that a brother of her father's "died in England".

A voyage that came to an end before the beckoning coast of England was

Above: In Lingsberg in Uppland two rune stones were set up by three brothers in memory of their father and grandfather who had taken two gelds in England. *Below:* Left. While he was still alive, Alle who lived in Väsby in Uppland had this rune stone raised in memory of himself. Right. One of two Sävsjö stones from Småland was raised in memory of Vråe who once held high office in Håkon jarl's court.

reached is spoken of on a rune stone from Husby-Lyhundra (Uppland): **tiarfʀ × uki ×urika × uk × uiki × uk × iukiʀ × uk × kiʀialmʀ × þiʀ bryþr × aliʀ × litu × risa × stin þina × iftiʀ × suin × bruþur × sin × saʀ × uarþ × tuþr a × iutlati × on skulti fara × til × iklanþs × kuþ × ialbi × ons at uk salu × uk × us muþiʀ × betr × þan an karþi til.** *Diarfʀ ok Orøkia ok Vigi ok Iogæiʀʀ ok Gæiʀhialmʀ, þæiʀ brøðr alliʀ letu ræisa stæin þenna æftiʀ Svæin, broður sinn. Saʀ varð dauðr a Iutlandi, hann skuldi fara til Ænglands. Guð hialpi hans and ok salu ok Guðs moðiʀ bætr þan hann gærði til.* "Djärv and Orökja and Vige and Joger and Gerhjälm, all these brothers had this stone raised in memory of Sven, their brother. He died in Jutland. He was on his way to England. May God and God's mother help his spirit and soul better than he deserved." The statement of particular interest in this context is: *Saʀ varð dauðr a Iutlandi, hann skuldi fara til Ænglands.*

Some archaeological discoveries of recent years throw a fascinating light on the contents of this inscription. The sites of two large fortified circular camps have been found in Jutland, one at Aggersborg on the north side of the Limfjord, the other at Fyrkat at the head of the Mariagerfjord. These great establishments were evidently military bases, built at the end of the tenth century and in use until the middle of the eleventh. Ships' crews from the whole of Scandinavia foregathered in these camps: in them the Vikings were quartered and trained and initiated into the great fraternity of the sea until at last under strong and resolute captains they sailed out into the North Sea towards the rich goals of France and England.

We know that Viking attacks on England were mounted from the Limfjord. Canute's great invasion fleet collected in its calm sheltered waters in 1015. Like so many others, Sven of the Husby-Lyhundra stone, tempted by tales of the Danegeld, had set off to join an enterprise against England early in the eleventh century. But when the longed-for moment came and the longships were running free with the Jutland coast astern, Sven was not on board—*Saʀ varð dauðr a Iutlandi*. He lies in a Jutish grave, perhaps at Aggersborg or Fyrkat.

A number of rune stones tell of historical events which were clearly well known at the time they were inscribed, but which we can unfortunately neither locate nor date with certainty. Thus we do not know, for example, what battle is meant by the Råda inscription (Västergötland): **+ þurkil ⁺₊ sati + stin + þasi + itiʀ + kuna + sun · sin + iʀ · uarþ + tuþr + i uristu + iʀ · bþiþus + kunukaʀ +** *Þorkell satti stæin þannsi æftiʀ Gunna, sun sinn. Eʀ varð dauðr i orrostu, eʀ barðus kunungaʀ.* "Torkel placed this stone in memory of Gunne, his son. He met death in battle when the kings fought." One is naturally tempted to guess that it was the sea-battle of Svöld in the year 1000, when Olav Tryggvason of Norway fought against Sven Forkbeard of Denmark and Olav the Swede. But we do not know.

A reference to a sea-battle on one of the rune stones at Fresta church

Above: Sven, commemorated by his brothers on the rune stone at Husby-Lyhundra church in Uppland, never reached England. He died in Jutland. *Below:* "... varð dauðr a Iutlandi ..."

(Uppland), which also dates from the beginning of the eleventh century, is equally obscure: **kunar × uk × sasur × þiʀ × litu × risa × stin × þina × iftiʀ × kiʀbiarn × faþur × sin × sun × uitkars × i × sua̲lunisi × on × trabu × nurminr × o kniri × asbiarnaʀ** *Gunnarr ok Sassurr þæiʀ letu ræisa stæin þenna æftiʀ Gæiʀbiorn, faður sinn, sun Vittkarls i Svalunæsi. Hann drapu norrmænnr a knærri Asbiarnaʀ.* "Gunnar and Sassur, they had this stone raised in memory of Gerbjörn, their father, son of Vittkarl in Svalnäs. Norwegians killed him on Åsbjörn's ship." It may have been in the battle of Svöld that Gerbjörn fell on board the *knarr* of the ship's captain Åsbjörn, but we must bear in mind that most events of the past have gone unchronicled. And when we consider the unusually good opportunities available in the Viking Age for losing one's life on board a ship, we must again admit the impossibility of putting the inscription's statement into any known historical context.

A battle of some importance was evidently fought at Gårdstånga in Skåne. The Forsheda stone (Småland) has this inscription: **: rhulf : auk : oskihl : riþu : stin þonsi : etiʀ : lifstin : fuþur : sin : es : uarþ : tuþr : : o : skonu : i : karþ : stokum : auk : furþu : o : : finhiþi** *Hrolfʀ ok Askell ræisþu stæin þannsi æftiʀ Lifstæin, faður sinn. Es varð dauðr a Skanøy i Garðstangum, ok førðu a Finnhæiði.* "Rolf and Äskil raised this stone in memory of Livsten, their father. He met death in Skåne at Gårdstånga. And they brought him to Finnheden." (On Finnveden see pp. 102 f.)

It has been maintained that this battle took place during Canute the Great's war against King Anund Jakob of Sweden and Olav the Saint of Norway, i.e.

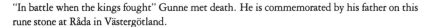

"In battle when the kings fought" Gunne met death. He is commemorated by his father on this rune stone at Råda in Västergötland.

This rune stone stands outside the church of Fresta in Uppland. It tells us that Gerbjörn was killed by Norwegians in a sea-battle.

during hostilities in Skåne in 1025—26. That is possible, even probable, and in that case Livsten also fell in battle "when the kings fought". But we can come no closer to the historical facts: the rune stone in memory of Livsten of Finnveden is the only source we have that tells of an action at Gårdstånga.

We seem to be on rather firmer ground when we come to identify the historical events that are reflected in the inscriptions on stones at Hällestad and Sjörup in Skåne. They give significant expression of the ideal of loyalty to leader. In considering the relationship between chieftain and retainer, it is illuminating to see how the dead leader is called "brother" by his men. On the stone at Hällestad we read: : **askil : sati : stin : þansi : iftiᴙ : tuka : kurms : sun : saᴙ : hulan : trutin : saᴙ : flu : aigi : at : ub : salum / satu : trikaᴙ: iftiᴙ : sin : bruþr stin : o : biarki : stuþan : runum : þiᴙ : / kurms : tuka : kiku : nistiᴙ** *Æskill satti stæin þannsi æftiᴙ Toka, Gorms sun, seᴙ hullan drottin.*

> *Saᴙ flo æigi*
> *at Upsalum.*
> *Sattu dræengiaᴙ*
> *æftiᴙ sinn broður*
> *stæin a biargi*
> *støðan runum.*
> *Þæiᴙ Gorms Toka*
> *gingu næstiᴙ.*

"Äskil placed this stone in memory of Toke, Gorm's son, his gracious lord.

> He fled not
> at Uppsala.
> 'Drængs' set up
> after their brother
> the stone on the rock,
> stayed with runes.
> To Toke Gorm's son
> they marched closest."

(The phrase *seᴙ hullan drottin* may be compared with the compound adj. ON *dróttinhollr*, "loyal to one's lord". Sighvatr Þórðarson used it in his *Bersǫglis-vísur*, "Frank-speaking verses", composed towards 1040:

> *Vask með gram, þeims gumnum*
> *goll bauð dróttinhollum . . .*

"I was with the king who proffered gold to lord-loyal men . . .")

The same battle at Uppsala is referred to on the Sjörup stone, where the inscription ends with this homage to the dead man: **saᴙ : flu : aki : at : ub : salum : an : ua : maþ : an : uabn : afþi**

> *Saᴙ flo æigi*   "He fled not
> *at Uppsalum*   at Uppsala
> *en va*   but struck
> *með hann vapn hafði.*   while he had weapon."

Toke, commemorated on the Hällestad stone in Skåne, took part in a famous fight at Uppsala at the end of the tenth century.

The battle mentioned in these inscriptions was very likely that great fight, famous in legend, which took place on the banks of the Fyris river at Uppsala sometime between 980 and 990. It is one of the most celebrated battles in early Scandinavian history, and King Erik of Sweden is supposed to have won his cognomen "the Victorious" because of the defeat he inflicted on his enemies on Fyris fields.

One of the five men named on the Högby stone (Östergötland) also appears to have died in this battle: · **feal** · **o** · **furi** · **frukn** · **treks** · **asmuntr**. *Fiall a Føri frøkn drængʀ Asmundr.* "Fell on Fyris plain ('Føret') the valiant 'dræng' Åsmund."

The Torsätra stone gives us concise information about another aspect of early history—the tributary status of the Gotlanders in relation to the Swedish king in the eleventh century: · **skuli** · **auk** · **folki** · **lata** · **reisa** · **þinsa** · **stein** · **iftʀ** · **broþur** · **sin** · **husbiorn** · **hn usiok** · **uti** · **þa þiʀ** · **kialt** · **toku** · **a kutlanti** *Skuli ok Folki lata ræisa þennsa stæin æftiʀ broður sinn Husbiorn. Hann vas siukʀ uti, þa þæiʀ giald toku a Gutlandi.* "Skule and Folke have this stone raised in memory of their brother, Husbjörn. He fell sick abroad, when they took tribute in Gotland." The stone was undoubtedly carved by Visäte, so the inscription can be dated to the 1060s or '70s.—A bloodstained affray on Gotland is referred to in the inscription on the Aspö stone (Södermanland), set up in memory of Björn, who "was killed on Gotland. He lost his life for his companions fled..."—**uaʀ trebin : a : kut : lanti : þy : lit : fiur · sit : fluþu : kankiʀ :**... *vaʀ drepinn a Gutlandi.*

Þy let fior sitt,
flyðu gængiʀ...

Swedish kings ruled in South Jutland for some decades in the early tenth century. Among the evidence which demonstrates the existence of this Swedish dominion are the two stones which Asfrid, Odinkar's daughter, had set up in memory of King Sigtrygg, Gnupa's son and hers.

The Swedish kings in South Jutland had their seat in Hedeby—the nodal point for Baltic and North Sea trade and, with Birka in Mälaren, Scandinavia's most important township. From the point of view of commercial policy and power, no place in the North was more rewarding—or more difficult—to rule

Left: This rune stone from Torsätra in Uppland was set up in memory of Husbjörn who "fell sick abroad, when they took tribute in Gotland". *Right:* On one of the rune stones at Grinda in Södermanland we read about a man who was in Greece and took his share of gold. The other was raised to commemorate a man who went to the west and took his share of the geld in England.

over. It is not surprising to find this famous name recorded on two rune stones in central Sweden commemorating men who died *i Hæiðaby*.

South of Hedeby, on the other side of the ramparts of the mighty Danevirke, lay the land of the Saxons. The frontier between the Scandinavian North and Saxland was marked by this great defensive wall, which extends across South Jutland at its narrowest point. Two rune stones in Södermanland preserve the memory of Viking forays against the Saxons. The Grinda inscription (cf. p. 80 above) mentions both Saxland and England: **: kriutkarþr : ainriþi : suniʀ : kiarþu : at faþur : snialan : kuþuiʀ uastr : a : aklati : kialti : skifti : burkiʀ : a : sahks : lanti : suti : karla :**

The Högby stone in Östergötland commemorates five brothers, one of them fell in battle on the banks of the river Fyris in Uppsala.

Griutgarðr, Æinriði, syniʀ	"Grytgård, Endride, sons,
giarðu at faður sniallan.	made it in memory of their bold father.
Guðveʀ vaʀ vestr a Ænglandi,	Gudve was west in England,
gialdi skifti.	took his share of geld.
Borgiʀ a Saxlandi	Townships in Saxland
sotti karla.	he attacked like a man."

The inscription of the Högby stone, mentioned above, deserves to be quoted in full. It offers striking evidence of the restlessness of the Viking Age, of the constant movement on many different routes, and of the heavy losses in men:

· þukir · resþi · stin · þansi · eftiʀ · asur · sin · muþur · bruþur · sin · iaʀ · eataþis · austr · i · krikum · / · kuþr · karl · kuli · kat · fim · suni · feal · o furi · frukn · treks · asmutr · aitaþis · asur · austr · i krikum · uarþ · o hulmi · halftan · tribin · kari · uarþ · atuti · auk · tauþr · bui · þurkil · rist · runaʀ ·

Þorgærðr ræisþi stæin þannsi æftiʀ Assur, moðurbroður sinn. Er ændaðis austr i Grikkum.

"Torgärd raised this stone in memory of Assur, her mother's brother. He died out east in Greece."

Goðr karl Gulli	"The good man Gulle
gat fæm syni:	had five sons:
fiall a Føri	by Fyris fell Åsmund,
frøkn drængʀ Asmundr,	the valiant 'dræng',
ændaðis Assurr	Assur died
austr i Grikkum,	out east in Greece,
varð a Holmi	Halvdan was
Halfdan drepinn.	on Borgholm (?) slain.
Kari varð **atuti.**	Kari was **atuti.**
Auk dauðr Boi.	Dead is Boe too."

Þorkell ræist runaʀ . "Torkel cut the runes."

Unfortunately, no certain interpretation of **uarþ · atuti** can be offered. The suggestion that the line means "Kåre died at Dundee" (in Scotland, that is) must be regarded as extremely dubious, even though it would provide suitable alliteration (*Dundee—dauðr*). Doubt must also attach to the proposal that we should read it as *at Uddi*—"Kåre was killed at Od".

The long-distance voyages of the Viking Age may perhaps be read out of the even briefer words inscribed on a whetstone found in 1940 at Timans in Roma (Gotland): **: ormiga : ulfua-r : krikiaʀ : iaursaliʀ : islat : serklat.** There are just six names on it: two personal names and four names of remote places, Greece,

Four geographical names on a whetstone from Roma on Gotland perhaps tell us where the owner had been.

Jerusalem, Iceland and Serkland. The inscription can be dated to the second half of the eleventh century.

The Högby stone, carved by Torkel at the beginning of the eleventh century, and the little Gotlandic whetstone can be taken as monuments that symbolise all those aspects of Viking Age activity we have so far reviewed.

THE HOMELAND IN THE LIGHT OF RUNIC INSCRIPTIONS

Naturally, the Swedish coasts were themselves also liable to attack from foreign fleets. The Bro stone (Uppland) gives us a glimpse of Swedish coastal defence organisation, of the watch that was kept against Viking raiders: **kinluk × hulmkis × tutiʀ × systiʀ × sukruþaʀ × auk × þaiʀa × kaus × aun × lit × keara × bru × þesi × auk × raisa × stain × þina × eftiʀ × asur × bunta sin × sun × hakunaʀ × iarls × saʀ × uaʀ × uikika × uaurþr × miþ × kaeti × kuþ × ialbi × ans × nu × aut × uk × salu** *Ginnlaug, Holmgæiʀs dottir, systiʀ Sygrøðaʀ ok þæiʀa Gauts, hon let gæra bro þessi ok ræisa stæin þenna æftir Assur, bonda sinn, son Hakonaʀ iarls. Saʀ vaʀ vikinga vǫrðr með Gæiti. Guð hialpi hans nu and ok salu.* "Ginnlög, Holmger's daughter, sister of Sygröd and of Göt, she had this 'bridge' made and this stone raised in memory of Assur, her husband, son of Håkon Jarl. He kept watch against Vikings with Geter. May God now help his spirit and soul." The inscription introduces us to two of the most distinguished among the high-born families of the Mälar region, known to us in two other inscriptions from the beginning of the eleventh century—the Ramsund rock and the Kjula stone.

A couple of words on a rune stone fragment from Giberga in Södermanland belong in the same context: (*þæir*) *gerðu skipvǫrð* "...they kept ship-watch".

I shall cite only one of the inscriptions from later times that provide historical information. It is on a handsome grave-slab in Lye church on Gotland. The long inscription reads: + þinna · sten : þa · lit · husfru · ruþvi · giera · yfir sin · bonda · iakop · i · managardum · sum skutin · uarþ · ihel · miþ · en : þyrsu · stin · af · uis · borh · þa · en · kunuung · erik · uar · bi · stallaþ · pa · þi · for · nemda · slot · en · þa · uar · liþit · af · guz · byrþ · fiurtan · hundraþ : ar · ok · ainu : ari · minna · þen : femtigi : ar · biþium · þet: et · guþ :

This rune stone at Bro in Uppland informs us of the watch kept against Viking raiders along the Swedish coast.

92

naþi · hanz · sial · ok · allum · krisnum · sialum : amen "Lady Rudvi then let this stone be made [to lie] over her husband, Jakob of Mannagården, who was shot to death by a cannon ball from Visborg, when King Erik was besieged in the aforesaid castle. And then fourteen hundred years and one year less than fifty years had passed since God's nativity. Let us pray that God have mercy on his soul and all Christian souls. Amen."

It is however not only of warfare, feats of arms and death at home and in distant lands that the Swedish rune stones can tell us. They can also throw light on peaceful trade and on the labours and aspirations of men and women in their local sphere, although of course we cannot expect them to bring us into living contact with the everyday existence of Viking Age people.

The Bjälbo stone was rasied in memory of a guild-brother near the ancient market-place Skänninge in Östergötland.

Trade was a prime mover in the dynamics of the Viking Age. A number of the rune stones described above were undoubtedly raised in memory of Swedish merchants who had sailed distant seas. Birka flourished for two hundred years as the centre for transit-trade between East and West. Later, Sigtuna took over the role of Sweden's commercial capital. Here the merchants established their guilds for mutual protection and aid.

Two of Sigtuna's many runic inscriptions well illustrate its commercial connections. One reads: **+ frisa : kiltar · letu · reisa · stein : þensa : eftiʀ · þur[kil · kilt]a · sin : kuþ : hialbi : ant · hans : þurbiurn : risti** *Frisa gildaʀ letu ræisa stæin þennsa æftiʀ Þorkil, gilda sinn. Guð hialpi and hans. Þorbiorn risti.* "The guild-brethren of the Frisians had this stone set up in memory of Torkel, their guild-brother. God help his soul. Torbjörn carved."—The other inscription is found on a boulder embedded in the ground in the middle of the town. It has a similar message: **× frisa : kil [tar : letu : rista : runar] : þesar : eftʀ: alboþ : felaha : sloþa : kristr : hia : helgi : hinlbi : ant : hans : þurbiun : risti** "The guild-brethren of the Frisians had these runes cut in memory of Albod, Slode's partner. Holy Christ help his soul. Torbjörn carved."

To these inscriptions, which give such interesting insight into the early history of these important social and commercial institutions, the guilds, may be added two more of a similar kind. Both these rune stones have come to light in Östergötland, and it is significant that the site of each is close to a notable commercial and cultural centre. One is situated at Bjälbo, near the ancient market-place, Skänninge, and the other is at Törnevalla, not far from Linköping.

The Bjälbo stone has this inscription: " 'Drængs' raised this stone in memory of Grep, their guild-brother." The Törnevalla stone, discovered in 1960, was put up by members of a guild "in memory of Dräng, Öger's son, their guild-brother"—*æftir Dræng, Øygæiʀs sun, gilda sinn.*

Like that of the Frisians in Sigtuna, these guilds in Östergötland must, it seems, have been guilds of merchants. The members of the "Bjälbo guild" and the "Törnevalla guild" were most probably well-to-do yeomen who engaged in trade as well as farming. It seems likely that these Swedish commercial guilds in the last part of the Viking Age were modelled on west European counterparts, even though associations of such a kind came into being early in the Norse world.

The farm-names recorded on rune stones also take us into our native country-side. Not a few farmers in the Mälar districts can be—and usually are—proud of

This grave-slab was made to lie over Jacob of Manngården's grave in Lye church on Gotland. He was killed at Visborg castle in 1449.

The Törnevalla stone was discovered not far from Linköping in Östergötland. It commemorates a guild-brother named Dräng.

the fact that the name of their farm is inscribed on the rune stone they have at home, standing somewhere close to the farmstead or on the slope that once, long ago, was the ancestral burial ground.

These runic records of place-names are of course the oldest in Sweden, and this lends them special interest. The rune stones show that for the most part the farms had the same names in ancient times as they have now.

In a number of cases the farm-name was evidently included in the inscription because it was felt important to indicate clearly where the ownership of the land lay. The rune stone then served a double purpose, acting both as a memorial and as a title-deed. It could remind the outside world of how the survivors or descendants had gained possession of their property.

The runic inscription at Nora (Uppland) may be regarded as such a title-deed —one that literally stands as firm as a rock: *Biorn, Finnviðaʀ sunn, let hǫggva hælli þessa æftiʀ Olæif, broður sinn. Hann varð svikvinn a Finnæiði. Guð hialpi and hans. Eʀ þessi byʀ þæiʀa oðal ok ættærfi, Finnviðaʀ suna a Ælgiastaðum.* "Björn, Finnvid's son, had this rock carved in memory of Olev, his brother. He was betrayed {i.e. treacherously killed} on Finnveden. God help his soul. This farm is their odal and family inheritance, the sons of Finnvid at Älgesta."

This elegant carving thus tells of Olev Finnvidsson's violent end on *Finnæiði*, now Finnveden, in southwest Småland. (On the name of this well-known district see pp. 102 f.) But it is the close of the inscription which particularly attracts our attention at this point.

The place meant by *þessi byʀ*, "this farm", is Nora, the site of the inscription. But the great farm of the sons of Finnvid, Älgesta (**o ilhiastaþum**), lies in Husby-Ärlinghundra parish, 30 km due north of Nora. There is no need to doubt the identification of this Älgesta as the family estate of the sons of Finnvid, for we find a rune stone there which says that "Björn, Finnvid's son, had the stone raised in memory of himself".

At Ågersta village (Uppland) there is a rune stone, inscribed by Balle, which serves as a boundary mark between two properties. The inscription says: "Vidhugse had this stone raised in memory of Särev, his noble father. He lived at Ågersta"—*Hann byggi Agurstaðum* (**han · byki · agurstam ·**).

Hiær mun standa	"Here shall stand
stæinn miðli byia.	the stone between farms.
Raði drængʀ	Let that 'dræng' read
þaʀ rynn se	who rune-wise is
runum þæim	those the runes
sum Balli risti.	that Balle carved."

A peculiar chain of inheritance is recorded on the rune-inscribed rock at Hillersjö (Uppland), where the passer-by is also exhorted to "read"—i.e. interpret—the runes. "Read the runes! Germund took Gerlög to wife when she was a maid. Later they had a son, before Germund was drowned. Afterwards the son died. Then she had Gudrik as her husband. He... {part of the inscription is destroyed, with the loss of about 25 runes]. Then they had children. Of them only a girl lived; she was called Inga. Ragnfast of Snottsta took her to wife. Afterwards he died and then the son. And the mother took the inheritance after her son. Inga afterwards had Erik as her husband. Then she died. Then Gerlög came into the inheritance after Inga, her daughter. Torbjörn Scald cut the runes." The Viking Age rules of inheritance that were applied in this case agree with the statutes of the Uppland Law, codified in 1296.

Ragnfast of Snottsta, i · **snutastaþum**, is known from four other inscriptions at home on his patrimonial estate. They were made in his memory by his widow, Inga, also mentioned in the Hillersjö inscription above. In one of the inscriptions we read: "Inga had the runes cut for Ragnfast, her husband. He alone owned this

The inscription on this rock at Nora in Uppland served a double purpose, as a memorial and as a title-deed.

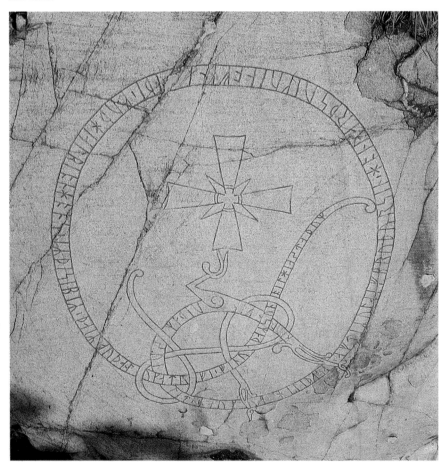

farm in succession to Sigfast, his father. God help their souls." In another of these Snottsta inscriptions we find a direct link with the one at Hillersjö: "Inga raised staff and stones in memory of Ragnfast, her husband. She came into the inheritance after her child."

The history of another inheritance is traced in the inscriptions on the two Hansta stones in Spånga parish (Uppland). The stones were put up in memory of the brothers, Ärnmund and Ingemund, who had died in Greece. The inscriptions read: *Gærðarr ok Iorundr lata ræisa þessa stæina æftiʀ systursyni sina Ærnmund ok Ingimund. Þessun mærki eʀu gar æftiʀ syni Inguʀ. Hon kam þæira at arfi, en þæiʀ brøðr kamu hænnaʀ at arfi, Gærðarr brøðr. Þæiʀ dou i Grikkium* "Gärdar and Jorund have these stones raised in memory of their sister's sons,

At Ågersta in Uppland there is a rune stone, which serves as a boundry mark between two properties.

In this inscription on the Malsta stone from Hälsingland, cut with stave-less runes, an ancient family can be traced through seven generations.

Ärnmund and Ingemund.—These memorials are made in memory of Inga's sons. She came into the inheritance after them [*viz.* Ärnmund and Ingemund], and the brothers—Gärdar and his brother—came into the inheritance after her. They [*viz.* Ärnmund and Ingemund] died in Greece."

So the sequence of inheritance had gone like this: Ärnmund and Ingemund had succeeded to the patrimonial estate on their father's death. They had then made the traditional journey to Greece, where they lost their lives. The inheritance then passed to their mother, Inga, and on her death it went to her brothers, Gärdar and Jorund. These, in gratitude, then raised the two rune stones to the memory of their nephews, dead in Greece.

We learn the names of some members of Swedish Viking Age families from these inscriptions at Hillersjö, Snottsta and Hansta. Sometimes we get to know a family through several generations.

This is particularly the case with the Malsta stone in Rogsta parish (Hälsingland). In this inscription we can trace an ancient family through seven generations. It must undoubtedly also have had a legal purpose. It is a significant fact, and one of no small interest to any student of Sweden's ancient culture, that this inscription is written in staveless runes. As noted on pp. 28 f. above, these runes might be called the shorthand of the ancients: they were developed for practical use, for records of various kinds, and only in rare and exceptional cases employed for memorial inscriptions on rune stones.

The Malsta stone bears this inscription: "Frömund raised this stone in memory of Rike-Gylve, Bräse's son. And Bräse was Line's son, and Line was Ön's son, and Ön was Ofeg's son, and Ofeg was Tore's son. Groa was Rike-

Gylve's mother, and she... and then Gudrun. Frömund, Rike-Gylve's son, cut these runes. We fetched this block of stone north in Balsten. Gylve acquired this district and also three estates farther north. He also acquired Lönnånger and afterwards Färdsjö."

Another remarkable stone from this point of view is at Sandsjö (Småland), on which six generations are counted: "Ärnvard had this stone raised in memory of Hägge, his father, and of Hära, his father, and Karl, his father, and Hära, his father, and Tegn, his father, and in memory of these five forefathers."

It is the Norseman's inborn interest in genealogy, clearly fully alive in ancient times, that we meet in these last inscriptions.

Just two or three more of the farm-names occurring in Viking Age inscriptions can be considered in this account. At Lövhamra in Skepptuna parish (Uppland) there is a rune stone set up in memory of **ulf × i lukobri**, undoubtedly to be read as *Ulf i Laughambri*. The rune stone's farm-name thus differs from the present *Löv*hamra. On the other hand, there can be no doubt whatever that the original form is the one that appears on the stone. The first element is the word *laug* "bath", found for example in the Scandinavian word for Saturday, *lördag* (< *laugardagr*), properly "bath-day". Later, when both the bathing-place there and the word *laug* had gone out of use, the farm-name was re-interpreted and turned into the inappropriate Lövhamra (*löv* is English 'leaf'). On one of the Skårby stones raised in memory of Tumme, it is said that "he owned Gusnava"—**iʀ ati × kuþis × snaba ×**. It is a farm lying some 10 km northwest of Ystad (Skåne).—Probably the Gotland market-place Boge is referred to on the Vidbo stone, set up to commemorate Vinaman: "he died in Boge"—**hon uarþ tauþr i buhi.**

Place-names of other kinds also occur here and there. The name of the lake Båven (Södermanland) is found on the Sund stone, set up on the shore of the stretch of water in which Vred was drowned: **han + turuknaþi + i + bagi + harmtauþ + mukin +** *Hann drunknaði i Bagi, harmdauð mykinn* "He drowned in Båven, a death that caused great grief".

Names of Swedish provinces and larger settlements also occur, often in a warlike context. Gotland is named several times. One instance is on the Torsätra stone, see pp. 87 f. above, and another on the Aspö stone (cf. p. 88), raised in memory of a man who *vaʀ drepinn a Gutlandi*—**uaʀ trebin : a : kut : lanti :** . On Östman Gudfastason's stone on Frösön we find the name of Jämtland: **han lit kristnạ eạtalạnt.** The Forsheda stone has both Skåne (**o skanu** *a Skanøy*) and "Finnheden" (**o : finhiþi** *a Finnhæiði*); see p. 84 above. Skåne recurs on the Ärja stone (Södermanland), which also supplies the oldest record we possess of the name of Kalmarsund. Of one of the men named the inscription says: *Varð uti drepinn i Kalmarna sundum, foru af Skanøy*—"He was killed out in Kalmarsund— **i · kalmarna · sutuma**—when they were going from Skåne (**afu · skani**)". In Snorri's *Heimskringla* we find forms which fully agree with the Runic Swedish pl. *Kalmarniʀ: Kalmarnir, Kalmarnar, Kalmarna-leiðangr.*

The Malsta stone itself is now in Hudiksvall Museum, but this replica has been placed on its original site.

Öresund occurs in the inscription on the Mejlby stone, put up by a father to commemorate his son who "died with Tore in Öresund"—**ias : tauþr uarþ : maþ : þuri : i : ura : suti.** And a rune stone on Bornholm was inscribed in memory of a man who "was killed in the battle at Utlängan" (off southeast Blekinge)—*i orrostu at Utlængiu.*

"Finned" must apparently be the earliest name for the district now called Finnveden, comprising the hundreds (*härader*) of Sunnerbo, Östbo and Västbo in the southwest corner of Småland. The sixth-century Gothic historian Jordanes mentions the inhabitants of Finnveden in his *De origine actibusque Getarum,* calling them *Finnaithæ.* It was, we recall, in Finnveden that Olev Finnvidsson

"Götrad made this monument in memory of Astrad, his father, best of kinsmen and of thegns who in times past lived in Finnveden" is the message of the Replösa stone.

was treacherously killed (see p. 97 on the Nora inscription): **han uarþ suikuin o finaiþi.** This important part of Småland is also named on the Replösa stone, which is in the Sunnerbo hundred and so belongs to Finnveden itself: **: kutraþr : karþi : kubl : þisi : iftiʀ : astraþ : faþur : sin : þan : frita : ak : þih : na : bistan : iʀ a : fin : iþi : forþum : ufaʀi** : *Gautraðr gærði kumbl þessi æftiʀ Astrað, faður sinn,*

> *þann frænda*
> *ok þegna bæztan,*
> *eʀ a Finnæiði*
> *forðum of væri.*

The man in memory of whom this stone was raised was killed in Kalmarsund on his way from Skåne.

"Götrad made these monuments in memory of Astrad, his father, best of kinsmen and of 'thegns' who in times past lived in Finnveden."

Another of these venerable Småland regional names is perhaps to be read on a stone found at Västerljung (Södermanland): **haunefʀ + raisti · at · kaiʀmar · faþur · sin + haa · iʀ intaþr · a · þiusti · skamals · hiak · runaʀ þaʀsi +** "Honäv raised it in memory of Germar, his father. He died in Tjust. Skamhals cut these runes."

It would be a valuable acquisition if this could be counted the earliest record we so far know of the name of this coastal district of Småland—one of the "small (tribal) lands" that make up the province. The name of the people of Tjust—the tribal name—appears in a much older source, Jordanes' *De origine actibusque Getarum* mentioned a few lines above. In a list of Swedish "nationes" he includes *theu(s)tes,* which can hardly mean anything but the inhabitants of Tjust. It must however be noted that Västerljung has a neighbouring parish called Tystberga, with a first element which appears to be the same word as Tjust. In Tystberga it may also represent an ancient district-name, and it might in consequence be this place in Småland whose name is preserved in the rune stone's *a Piusti.*

It is a local settlement-name of this kind, this time in Södermanland, which occurs on the Aspa stone, found in 1937 near the old assembly place of Rönö hundred. Two Södermanland magnates have their epitaphs on the stone: **ostriþ : lit : [k]ira : kum[bl : þ]usi : at : anunt : auk : raknualt : sun : sin : / : urþu : ta[uþi]ʀ : i : tan [mar]ku : uaʀu : rikiʀ : o rauniki : ak : snialastiʀ : i : suiþiuþu** *Astrið let gæra kumbl þausi at Anund ok Ragnvald, sun sinn.*

> *Urðu dauðir i Danmarku,*
> *vaʀu rikiʀ a Rauningi*
> *ok sniallastiʀ i Sveþiuðu.*

"Astrid had these monuments made in memory of Anund and Ragnvald, her son.

> They died in Denmark,
> were men of rank in Röninge,
> and swiftest of deed in Sweden."

The Astrid who set up this imposing memorial was thus wife of Anund and Ragnvald was their son. The inscription tells us that they lived *a Rauningi.* In all probability this was one of the old principal settlements in Södermanland; **rauniki** appears to be related to the name of the *Rönö* hundred (OSw. *Røna hundare*) and the parish-name, *Røntuna* (now *Runtuna*).

In this connection it is of interest to consider a place-name, which has caused problems, recorded in *Ynglingatal* and Snorri's *Ynglinga saga*: *á Ræningi.* In the saga (ch. 39) Snorri describes how Ingjald the Ill-doer burnt to death Granmar, king of Södermanland, in a house on Selaön, and in the following chapter he says that Ingjaldr then stayed *a Ræningi: Ingjaldr konungr var þá staddr á Ræningi at veizlu.* It may be worth noting that one of the manuscripts, the so-called *Jöfraskinna* (AM 33 fol.) has the spelling *rauningi.* The identification of this important place has long been discussed and it appears that the Aspa stone's **a rauniki** could help towards a solution. The stone was sunk in the ground at the Rönö hundred's old assembly site in a parish rich in antiquities, among them the biggest grave-mound in Södermanland. May not *a Rauningi* in the Aspa inscription be the very place referred to in *Ynglingatal* and by Snorri?

Left: This monument was made in memory of a father and his son, who both died in Denmark. It was set up near the assembly place of Rönö hundred. *Right:* This rune stone is one of four practically identical ones that were set up by Jarlabanke's bridge in Täby, Uppland.

Peaceful occupations

If we dare judge by the information imparted by rune stones, there were three kinds of peaceful public works undertaken in the home-districts that were of special significance: clearing roads, building bridges, and laying out assembly or thing places.

Bridge-building is mentioned particularly often, carried out to commemorate dead kinsfolk in this world and to ease their passage in the next. This custom was undoubtedly connected with the activity of the missionary church in Sweden. Roads that were serviceable in all weathers were essential if people were to come to God's house. To build bridges and to clear tracks through difficult terrain thus became good works, which were believed to be efficacious in helping souls through the searching fires of purgatory. In this way the eleventh century in Sweden was a road-building epoch.

In runic inscriptions the word "bridge" usually means a causeway over marshland or a stone-laid ford over watercourses crossing important roads.

106

Above: Jarlabanke's bridge in Täby, Uppland. *Below:* On a cliff-face just by the road in Södertälje one can read that Holmfast had the road cleared.

Despite radical changes in the communication network, there are still many places in Sweden today where the main road crosses the "bridge" that was first built in the Viking Age. An inscription in Södertälje, on a cliff-face just by the road, reads: **hulfastr lit × braut × ryþia × auk × bro kiara iftiʀ gamal × faþur × sin × sum × byki : nesby × kuþ × hialbi ant hans aystain** *Holmfastr let braut ryðia ok bro gæra æftir Gamal, faður sinn, sum byggi Næsby. Guð hialpi and hans! Øystæinn.* "Holmfast had the road cleared and the bridge made in memory of Gammal, his father, who lived in Näsby. God help his soul. Östen [carved]."

The most famous of all these rune-stone causeways is Jarlabanke's at Täby (Uppland). As far as we can tell, Jarlabanke put up four rune stones by his bridge, two facing each other at the north end and two at the south end. The bridge was also flanked by smaller standing-stones (ON *bautasteinar*), without runes on them. The length of the causeway was about 150 m, its width 6.5 m.

All four rune stones have practically identical inscriptions, which is naturally a pity from our point of view: **× iarlabaki × lit × raisa × staina × þisa × at sik × kuikuan × auk bru × þisa × karþi × fur ont × sina × auk ain ati × alan × tabu × kuþ hialbi ont hans** *Iarlabanki let ræisa stæina þessa at sik kvikvan, ok bro þessa gærði fyr and sina, ok æinn atti allan Tæby. Guð hialpi and hans!* "Jarlabanke had these stones raised in memory of himself in his lifetime. And he made this bridge for his soul. And alone he owned the whole of Täby. God help his soul."

This was undoubtedly one of Sweden's most impressive rune-stone bridges, rivalled only by a roadway at the Badelunda assembly place—see p. 125 below.

A rune stone at Årby in Lena parish (Uppland), originally put up as a road sign on the banks of the river Fyris, has this inscription **nasi × auk : þair : bruþr : raistu : stain : þisa × aftir : iarl : faþur : sin : kuþan : auk : bru : kus : þaka × kiarþu ×** *Nasi ok þæiʀ brøðr ræistu stæin þennsa æftir Iarl, faður sinn goðan, ok bro Guðs þakka gærðu.* "Nase and his brothers raised this stone in memory of Jarl, their noble father. And they made the bridge to please God." The expression *gæra bro Guðs þakka* (Deo gratias) also occurs on a Norwegian rune stone discovered in 1972. On the language of the missionary age see pp. 111, 112 f. below.

The phrase *(til) guðs þakka* is well known in medieval Norwegian and Icelandic, "to God's pleasure", often used of a work of Christian charity. It will suffice to quote an article in the early tithe laws of Iceland, which also illuminates the interest of churchmen in "bridges" and ferries: *þat fé þarf eigi til tíundar at telia, er áðr er til guðs þakka lagit, hvárt sem þat er til kirkna lagit eða til brúa eða til sáluskipa*—"that property need not be counted for the tithe which has already been contributed *til guðs þakka*—i.e. to works pleasing to God—whether to churches or bridges or charity-boats".

Another of the many "bridge" inscriptions in Uppland deserves notice. It is cut on the natural rock-face at Näs in Frösunda parish, and here again the motive of

Christian piety is clearly in evidence: **lefstein · lit kera · siʀ · til · sialu · botar · ok · sini kunu · ikirun · ok · sinum · sunum · iarntr · ok · nikulas · ok · luþin · broaʀ** *Lifstæinn let gæra seʀ til sialubotaʀ ok sinni kunu Ingirun ok sinum sunum Iarundr ok Nikulas ok Luðin broaʀ.* "Livsten had the bridges made for his soul's health and for that of Ingerun, his wife, and of his sons, Jarund and Niklas and Luden."

A splendid bridge-memorial once stood at Sälna (Uppland). We can feel the bridge-builders' pride in their work as we read: *Øystæinn ok Iorundr ok Biorn þæir brøðr ræisþu..., faður sinn. Guð hialpi hans and ok selu, forgefi hanum sakaʀ ok syndiʀ.*

> *Æi mun liggia*
> *með aldr lifiʀ*
> *bro harðslagin,*
> *bræið æft góðan.*
> *Svæinaʀ gærðu*
> *at sinn faður.*
> *Ma æigi brautaʀ kuml*
> *bætra verða.*

"Östen and Jorund and Björn, those brothers raised [this stone in memory of...], their father. May God help his spirit and soul, forgive him offences and sins. Always will lie / while mankind lives / the bridge firm-founded / broad after the noble man. / The boys made it / in memory of their father. / No road-monument / can be made better."

On a boulder at Runby in Ed parish, located at an important point in the network of Uppland waterways, are two inscriptions, which read as follows: **· ikriþ ᛙ lit · laþbo · kiara · auk · stain · hakua · eftir ikimar bota sin · auk · eftar · tan · auk · eftir · baka · suni · sina ᛙ þaiʀ byku ᛙ i rynby ᛙ auk ᛙ bo atu ᛙ kristr · ialbi ᛙ salu · þair[a] ᛙ þit skal ᛙ at minum · mana ᛙ miþan · min lifa** "Ingrid had the *laðbro* made and the stone cut in memory of Ingemar, her husband, and of Dan and of Banke, her sons. They lived in Runby and owned the farm. Christ help their souls. It shall stand in memory of the men as long as mankind lives."

The *laðbro* (**laþb[r]o**—the first element is ON *hlað*-) was probably a quay or jetty for loading vessels, an amenity which must have been of great importance to the inhabitants of this central district.

The most usual verb in the prayer uttered for the soul of the dead is *hialpa* "help", but others occur, e.g. *letta* "lighten, relieve". The Gryta stone (Uppland) has an inscription which says: "Tjälve made the bridge in memory of Bolla, his daughter. Alle and Olev had [the stone] cut in memory of Tjälve, their father, and Inga in memory of her husband. God give relief to their souls." The last part of this reads: **ika + at + uer sin + kuþ + liti + sal þaira.**

The Sälna stone was a bridge monument set up by sons in memory of their father.

liti is the third sg. subj. (optative) of the verb *letta*. It may be noted that **uer** represents the archaic word *verr* "man, husband" (cognate with Latin *vir*), which in its second sense was early replaced by *boandi, bondi* (usual on rune stones) and fell out of general use in its first. This old common Germanic noun in the sense of "man, human being" is found e.g. in ON *verǫld,* OE *weorold,* modern Sw. *värld,* Engl. *world.*

As was mentioned earlier, the modern main roads of Sweden are in many places bordered by rune stones that tell us who first built the way on which we now travel. But some stones are also located in places where traces of an ancient path are now only to be found with difficulty, among rocks and brushwood. In this way the siting of rune stones can sometimes give information about the land routes of the Viking Age, once important but now otherwise disappeared.

Another work of general public benefit, also intended to make travelling easier, was the building of *sæluhus,* "hospices, shelters". Such huts for the use of weary and weather-beaten travellers have been found in a number of districts, where the roads lie far from the settlements.

A rune stone, unfortunately damaged, at Karberga in Funbo parish (Uppland) bears witness to this custom: **ainkriþ ✕ auk ✕ inkikir · litu ✕ risa ✕ stin · auk ᛁ kera ᛁ aur ᛁ... sunti ᛁ iftiʀ ᛁ þuri ᛁ faþur sin ᛁ þur... t ᛁ kira · siluaus ᛁ iftʀ ᛁ ink[iþu]ru ✕ kunu · sina ᛁ auk ᛁ iftʀ...** "Ingrid and Ingegärd had the stone set up and the ford made in the channel in memory of Tore, their father. Tore had the hospice built in memory of Ingetora, his wife, and in memory of..."

The word **siluaus** is naturally an error for *siluhus.* The daughters **litu... kera ᛁ aur** in memory of their father; *gæra aur* means "to make a (gravel) bank", i.e. a causeway or ford; cf. ON *aurr,* m. "mud, clay", *eyrr,* f. "gravel bank, spit", modern Icel. *eyri* (frequent in place-names), Sw. *ör.* Another rune stone, found in 1973, uses the same expression, *gæra aur,* in recording that in memory of the dead a crossing was made over a difficult watercourse.

On a rune stone at Gryta in Kulla parish (Uppland) and on another in Aspö church in Södermanland it says that the surviving members of the family have had built **likhus : auk : bru**—*likhus ok bro.* The combination of the two words may make it tempting to identify the first element in *likhus* as *likn* "mercy"— although a compound *liknhus* is not found elsewhere—and to take it as meaning "house of mercy", another form of *sæluhus* "hospice". A different and preferable interpretation can however be offered.

The word *likhus* may mean literally "corpse-house" (cf. *lik* with the first element in English "lyke-wake", "lich-gate"), and, if so, it could denote a monument in the shape of a little house built over the grave. Such "grave-houses" have an ancient Christian tradition behind them, but it will be enough here just to mention their appearance in the early Germanic world. A statute in the laws of the Salic Franks says: "If anyone damages the house in the form of a basilica which has been set up over a dead man, let him pay thirty solidi in atonement."

One would presume that Viking Age "corpse-houses" in Sweden were made of wood, which perished as time passed. We know in fact that the custom of erecting little wooden houses over graves survived for hundreds of years in Sweden, and such buildings, so-called *gravrord (-rol, -ror),* were still common in the eighteenth century.

If this interpretation of *likhus* is correct, we have interesting information concerning Viking Age burial customs. These would be edifices in wood corresponding to the so-called Eskilstuna sarcophagi and other coffin-shaped grave monuments in stone. Since many of the latter have runes on them, I shall return to them later.

In connection with these laudable acts, bearing witness as they do to a public-spirited Christianity, it is appropriate to cite a few inscriptions whose mode of expression is characteristic of the missionary age in Sweden.

The interesting phrase, "to die in white clothes", occurs on seven Uppland rune stones, the last of them found in 1972. The Amnö stone says: "Ingelev had this stone raised in memory of Brune, her husband. He died in Denmark in white clothes. Balle carved." *Hann varð dauðr a Danmarku i hvitavaðum.* The Torsätra inscriptions reads: *Unna let ræisa þennsa stæin æftiʀ sun sinn Øystæin, sum do i hvitavaðum. Guð hialpi salu hans* "Unna had this stone raised in memory of her son, Östen, who died in white clothes. God help his soul." The Molnby stone has: "Holmlög and Holmfrid had the stones raised in memory of Faste and Sigfast, their sons. They died in white clothes." *Þæiʀ dou i hvitavaðum.* The Håga stone in Bondkyrka parish was put up by parents in memory of their son. He died *i hvitavaðum i Danmarku.*

The *hvitavaðiʀ,* "white clothes", baptismal robes, were worn by the convert at his baptism and for a week afterwards. The Upplanders in whose memory this group of rune stones was put up were thus baptised on their deathbed. It is the missionary period, the age of conversion, that we encounter in these inscriptions—their language is the language of the early church in Scandinavia, and

The so-called "Skrivar stone" from Skoghall in Södermanland is a large boulder with the inscription on one side. It is pictured here from a sketch made at the end of the nineteenth century by O. Hermelin.

those who set up the stones found consolation in the knowledge that their close kinsmen had escaped eternal punishment by accepting baptism as their last hour drew near.

It is typical that two of the dead men named in these inscriptions are said to have been baptised in Denmark. Voyages by Swedish men to countries where the new faith had been long established—England, Greece, Denmark, Saxland—were naturally of great significance for the introduction of Christianity in Sweden itself.

The language of the missionary age is already to be found on rune stones from the beginning of the eleventh century. The prayer formula which the sons of Ulv of Skålhamra had inscribed on his monument is extremely illuminating (Risbyle, Täby parish): *Ulfkætill ok Gyi ok Unni þæiʀ letu ræisa stæin þenna æftiʀ Ulf, faður sinn góðan. Hann byggi i Skulhambri. Guð hialpi hans and ok salu ok Guðs móðiʀ, le hanum lius ok paradis* "God and God's mother help his spirit and soul, grant him light and paradise".

This prayer for the gift of heavenly light and paradise to the soul of the dead man is found on two other stones, one in Uppland and one on Bornholm.

The Uppland stone stands at Folsberga in Vallby parish. The inscription ends with the prayer: **+[kr]istr + lati kumo + ot + tumo + i lus yk baratisi + yk i þon em + besta + krisnum +** *Kristr lati koma and Tumma i lius ok paradisi ok i þann hæim bæzta kristnum* "May Christ let Tumme's soul come into light and paradise and into the world best for Christians".

On the Bornholm stone (Klemensker 1) the formula is found twice. The second reads: **kristr : hialbi : siolu : auþbiarnar : auk : kuniltar : auk : santa mikel : i lius : auk : baratis** "Christ and Saint Michael help the souls of Ödbjörn and Gunnhild into light and paradise".

The celestial light also occurs in an inscription in Östergötland, on the Kimstad stone, put up by Sven and his brothers in memory of their father. It ends: **kuþ × hialbi × aut × has × auk × kus × muþir × i × lius ×** "God and God's mother help his soul into light".

The inscriptions just quoted indicate that the missionary church in Scandinavia used a relatively uniform language in its preaching. We may have a suspicion that the task of the missionary in Sweden was an arduous one: Valhall had to be exchanged for *paradis*, Thor and mysterious magic charms had to be replaced by God and God's mother, Christ and Saint Michael. It was a change of old currency for a new Christian coinage.

St Michael is invoked on the Ängby stone in Knivsta parish (Uppland) and the fine Hogrän stone on Gotland (as well as on three Bornholm stones and another from Lolland). The Ängby inscription has: **: mihel : kati : at : hans** *Mihel gætti and hans* "Michael take care of his soul", while on the Hogrän stone the prayer to the "weigher of souls" reads: **santa mikel hie[lbi ant h]ans**.

Odin, god of strife, once saw to the conveyance of dead heroes to Valhall—now the archangel Michael, captain of the heavenly host, has inherited his role and conducts Christian souls to "light and paradise".

The inscription on a handsome grave-slab in Tofta church (Gotland), carved at the end of the twelfth century, calls on one of the apostles to intercede for the soul of the dead man: **saktus barþolimeus irni miskunaʀ sialu roþurms** "May Saint Bartholomew obtain mercy for Rodorm's soul".

The inscription on a stone in Västergötland (Vg 186) ends with this supplication: *Guð hialpi salu hans ok Guðs moðiʀ, hæilagʀ Kristr i himinriki* "God and God's mother help his soul, holy Christ in heaven". Two other stones in the

The inscription on the Risbyle stone prays for "light and paradise" for the deceased's soul.

114

same province (Vg 105, 122) have an appeal to the Blessed Virgin: "God help his soul and holy Saint Mary". A lost gravestone once in Sparlösa churchyard had a runic inscription which ended "May his soul have heaven's joy. Amen"—*Hans sal hafi himinglæði. Amen.*

Another prayer formula, one which also shows a truly Christian frame of mind, is found on a number of rune stones, most of them set up in the first decades of the eleventh century. The Eggeby stone in Spånga parish (Uppland) may serve as an example: *Ragnælfʀ let gærva bro þessi æftiʀ Anund, sun sinn góðan. Guð hialpi hans and ok salu bætr þæn hann gærði til.*

"May Christ let Tumme's soul come into light and paradise and into the world best for Christians" is a prayer that ends the inscription on the Uppland Folsberga stone.

115

Munu æigi mærki
mæiri verða.

Moðir gærði æftiʀ sun sinn æiniga.

"Ragnälv had this bridge made in memory of Anund, her noble son. May God help his spirit and soul better than he deserved (**kuþ [× hil]bi × ons × ant × uk × salu × bitr × þan × on krþi × til ×**). No memorials will be greater. The mother made it for her only son." Slight variations on the same theme occur elsewhere: *Guð biargi sel hans bætr þæn hann hafʀ til gært* "God save his soul better than he deserved" (Brössike, Södermanland). On the Lilla-Lundby stone (Södermanland) it has this form: *Guð hialpi sal hans bætr þæn hann kunni til gærva* "God help his soul better than he knew how to deserve it".

In these petitions we must naturally see the humble hope that God will let mercy temper justice when the time comes to pass sentence on a poor and sinful creature. Such expressions must of course not be taken—as they recently have been—to mean that the dead man was a heathen or a particularly bad Christian. It is Christian humility which here speaks in the rune stone's voice. The formula has the same significance as the Sälna stone's supplication for forgiveness of the dead man's "offences and sins" (p. 109 above).

The end of the inscription on a stone found a few years ago in Uppsala deserves to be quoted in this context: *Guð signi oss, gumna valdr, hæilagʀ drottinn* "May God bless us, ruler of men, holy lord".

Of the people who raised these last-named monuments we might use the words that stand as Fare's memorial on the Källbyås stone (Västergötland): *Saʀ hafði goða tro til Guðs* "He had good faith in God".

The rune stones show in a variety of ways what important changes Christianity brought about in the social life of the Viking Age. Undoubtedly, one of the most radical changes was that the dead man was now to be buried in the consecrated ground of the churchyard, separated from his kin. He was no longer to lie in his grave on the slopes by the homestead where his ancestors lay.

An archaic provision in the church-section of the Uppland Laws leaves a deep impression of the cleavage this meant between old custom and new faith: "No one shall sacrifice to idols and no one shall put trust in groves or stones. All shall honour the church, thither all shall go, both the quick and the dead, coming into the world and leaving it"—*Allir skulu kirkiu dyrkæ, þit skulu allir, baþi quikkir ok døþir, komændi ok farændi i wæruld ok aff.* Venerable custom and family tradition were broken, and the ecclesiastical sections of the provincial laws enunciated the new obligations. (As a point of interest it may be recalled that the earliest legal provision preserved in Old Swedish is found incised in runes on a ring of forged iron that now belongs to Forsa church in Hälsingland; cf. p. 37 above.)

On this grave slab in Tofta church on Gotland one of the apostles is called on to intercede for the soul of Rodorm.

The new burial customs are reflected in one or two runic inscriptions. The Bogesund stone (Uppland) gives us one testimony: "Gunne and Åsa had this stone raised and (made this) coffin of stone in memory of... their son. He died at Ekerö. He is buried in the churchyard (a[n · i]ʀ · krafin · i · kirikiu · karþi ·). Fastulv cut the runes. Gunne raised this slab of rock." It is interesting to observe that in this transition period a rune stone was evidently set up in the ancestral cemetery at home, while a more ecclesiastical sort of monument was provided in the churchyard at Ekerö.

A rune stone stands at Bjärby bridge in Runsten parish (Öland), raised in memory of Fastulv by his wife and sons. From it we learn that *hann eʀ grafinn i kirkiu*. This must, it seems, mean that he had his grave inside the church itself, a very honorific place both then and now. Burial in consecrated ground is probably also indicated by the inscription on a rune stone, unfortunately damaged, from the ruin of St Pers (Peter's) church in Sigtuna. It ends by saying that the stone was set up by a man *sem hana førði til Sigtunum*. The dead person, a woman, seems thus to have been brought for burial in Sigtuna, at this time the stronghold of the missionary church in Uppland.

Left: The most northerly rune stone in Sweden stands on Frösön in Jämtland. Its inscription tells of the conversion of a whole province. *Right:* The Velanda stone in Västergötland was put expressly under Thor's protection.

Rune stones can thus tell us that churches existed in Sweden in the latter part of the Viking Age, though of course they are not our only sources of information about this early church-building.

It should be observed at this point that the change in burial customs may not always have been so deeply felt after all. The fact is that in a surprising number of cases the site chosen for the new enclosed churchyard adjoins some ancient family burial ground with all its traditional associations. In such cases, perhaps, the break in custom did not seem so definitive, at any rate for the family on whose land the church was built.

The conversion of a whole province, round about 1020–30, finds unambiguous record on the stone that stands on Frösön (Jämtland): **austmąþr kuþfastaʀ sun · lit rai... þina aukirua bru þisauk h[ąn li]t kristną eątaląnt ąsbiurn kirþi bru triun raist auk tsain runąʀ þisaʀ** "Östman, Gudfast's son, had this stone raised and this bridge made, and he had Jämtland made Christian. Åsbjörn made the bridge. Tryn and Sten cut these runes."

It seems likely that the conversion of Jämtland was the result of a decision taken at the assembly of the Jämtlanders, where Östman perhaps held office as law-man. In that case, we should have a parallel, on a modest scale, to the

The man in memory of whom one of the Källby ås stones was raised had "good faith in God". The two rune stones stand on either side of the road.

momentous decision of the Icelandic Althing, when this national assembly adopted Christianity in the year 1000, not many decades before the conversion of Jämtland.

Denmark had become Christian some time earlier, probably *c.* 960 or not long after, as is shown by the famous Jelling stone: "King Harald commanded these monuments to be made in memory of Gorm, his father, and of Tyre, his mother—that Harald who won all Denmark and Norway and made the Danes Christian".

Information preserved on contemporary rune stones thus enables us to draw some conclusions concerning the advance of Christianity in Sweden. Christian influence is also readily discernible in the personal names on the stones, which even in the missionary period show many new names of Christian provenance alongside the traditional pagan stock—Johan, Botvid, Nikulas and others.

One scans the inscriptions in vain for any evidence of violent conflict between the old faith and the new. On the contrary, they give the impression that the conversion was a rather tranquil process. From the transition period between heathendom and Christianity we have only one Swedish inscription which invokes a pagan deity. The Velanda stone (Västergötland) was set up by Tyrvi in memory of her husband, Ogmund, and it was put expressly under Thor's protection. The inscription, probably carved about the year 1000, ends: **þur : uiki** *Þorr vigi* "May Thor consecrate".

Inscribed grave monuments and other memorials with runes on them give us valuable information about the period that followed the eleventh-century missionary age itself. We shall come back to these in a later section.

Rune stones at assembly places

I have mentioned certain works of public benefit, undertaken to the glory of God and to the advantage of souls in the next world. A work that also met a social need was the laying-out of an assembly site, a thing place.

Modern building has fortunately not yet disturbed the thing place at Bällsta in Vallentuna parish (Uppland). Two rune stones stand there, with an inscription that begins on the one and continues on the other: **[ulfkil ·] uk · arkil · uk · kui · þiʀ · kariþu · iar · þikstaþ · [m]unu · iki mirki · maiʀi · uirþa · þan · ulfs · suniʀ · iftiʀ · kir [þu · snial]iʀ · suinaʀ · at · sin · faþur ristu · stina · uk · staf · uan · uk · in · mikla · at · iartiknum uk kuriþi · kas at · uiri · þu mon i krati · kiatit lata kunar ik stin**

Ulfkell ok Arnkell ok Gyi þæiʀ gærðu hiar þingstað.

"Ulvkel and Arnkel and Gye, they made here a thing place.

Munu æigi mærki	"There shall no mightier
mæiʀi verða,	memorials be found
þan Ulfs syniʀ	than those Ulv's sons
æftiʀ gærðu,	set up after him,
snialliʀ svæinaʀ,	active lads
at sinn faður.	after their father.
Ræistu stæina	They raised the stones
ok staf unnu	and worked the staff
auk inn mikla	also, the mighty one,
at iartæiknum.	as marks of honour.
Auk Gyriði	Likewise Gyrid
gats at veri.	loved her husband.
Þy man i grati	So in mourning
getit lata.	she will have it mentioned.
Gunnarr hiogg stæin.	Gunnar cut the stone."

What interests us especially at this point is that Ulv's sons laid out an assembly place on this beautiful and convenient site by the shore of the Vallentunasjö, where the rune stones stand. As far as we can see, however, the thing place, with its "mighty staff" and rune stones, remained in use for only a few decades—a surprising conclusion but unavoidable if we are to accept the evidence of another rune stone in the same parish. This is the Jarlabanke stone at Vallentuna church, with an inscription cut on both sides, one of which reads:

× **Iarlabaki** × **lit raisa** × **stain** × **þina** × **at sik** × **kuikuan** × **auk** × **þinkstaþ** × **þina** × **karþi** × **auk** × **ain ati** × **alt huntari** × **þita** × *Iarlabanki let ræisa stæin þenna at sik kvikvan, ok þingstað þenna gærði, ok æinn atti alt hundari þetta.*

We thus learn the interesting facts that in his lifetime Jarlabanke "made this thing place" and "alone owned the whole of this hundred". The phrasing suggests that Jarlabanke's thing place was intended to serve the whole Vallentuna hundred. The recorded Uppland laws say that there should be one assembly site in each hundred.

In passing it should be noted that Jarlabanke's claim to own the whole hundred may strike us as an exaggeration. He was probably the local magnate or perhaps the king's bailiff in charge of the Vallentuna district. It is certainly obvious that he was one of the leaders of the Vallentuna assembly.

Jarlabanke's establishment of a new thing place, at no great distance from the one laid out only twenty or thirty years earlier at Bällsta, might be explained in the following way. Jarlabanke has now become the most powerful man in the district. He could hardly preserve his equanimity as he entered the thing place at Bällsta, where the rune stones and "mighty staff" (*stafʀ hinn mikli*) would

The thing place at Bällsta in Uppland was laid out by sons to commemorate their father. The two rune stones tell us about it.

constantly remind him—and everyone else there—of the Skålhamra family who before his time were the greatest and most influential landowners in the locality. We know Ulv of Skålhamra from the clear witness of a number of rune stones. There is good reason to suppose that Jarlabanke was all too jealous of his own reputation to be able to tolerate, before his very eyes at the assembly place, the sight of the proud poem which the sons of Ulv had inscribed in their father's honour. No one was more concerned than Jarlabanke to look after his own obituary by means of rune-inscribed monuments; no one took such pains as he to preserve the memory of his own greatness. We can only agree that he was successful in his aim of preserving his name for posterity to admire.

A great "staff" or pole had been raised on the thing place at Bällsta in memory of Ulv. This custom is also attested in a number of other inscriptions. On the Vreta stone (Uppland) it says: **inka · raisti · staf · auk · staina · at · raknfast · bonta · sin · han · kuam · at · arfi barn · sins ·** "Inga raised staff and stones in memory of Ragnfast, her husband. He came into the inheritance of his child". It is possibly the same custom that is implied in the Fyrby inscription (Södermanland): **setu : stain : auk : stafa : marga** "They placed the stone and many staves..."

On a rune stone that once did service in the doorway of the now ruined church at Stora Ryttern (Västmanland) occur the words: "Gudlev placed staff and these stones in memory of Slagve, his son..."

This custom is described and light thrown on it from an unexpected quarter—in a source that is totally different in kind and about a century older than these rune stones. During his travels in Russia in 921–2 the Arabian diplomat, Ibn Fadlan, had the opportunity of witnessing at first hand the funeral of a Norse chieftain. When Ibn Fadlan arrived, the chieftain's ship had already been dragged ashore and preparations for the funeral ceremonies begun. When they were complete, the dead man's nearest kinsman first kindled the funeral pyre and then everyone helped to make it burn. In less than an hour the ship and the dead man had been reduced to ashes. Then on the place where the ship, dragged up out of the water, had stood, something like a circular mound of earth was thrown up. In the middle of the mound they erected a thick pillar of birchwood, and on it they cut the dead man's name and the name of the king of the Rus. Then they went their way.—There seems little doubt but that the birchwood pillar in Ibn Fadlan's account corresponds to the "staff" mentioned on rune stones. The alliterative phrase of the inscriptions, "staff and stones", evidently refers to a long-standing traditional custom.

An assembly place must, of course, have been a distinguished site for a rune stone. It had a central position in the district and all the members of the assembly had its inscription before their eyes. The grand Kjula stone stands on

Jarlabanke, who was a rich Upplander in Täby, made a thing place not to commemorate a dead relative but in honour of himself while he was still alive.

At the assembly site at Aspa in Södermanland Tora had two rune stones set up in memory of her husband. On this stone we read that it stands on the thing place.

the Rekarne thing place, while it was on the assembly site at Aspa (Södermanland) that Tora set up the rune stone that commemorates her husband, Öpir,
who had fought *vestarla*:

: stain : saʀ : si : stanr : at ybi : o þik : staþi : at : þuru : uar

Stæinn saʀsi	"This stone
standr at Øpi	stands after Öpir,
a þingstaði,	on the thing place
at Þoru ver . . .	after Thora's man."

The finest rune stone in Västmanland stands on the thing place at Badelunda.
We may take it for granted that the men whose names are recorded on it
belonged to the greatest family in the neighbourhood at the beginning of the
eleventh century. The inscription reads:

**× fulkuiþr × raisti × staina × þasi × ala × at × sun × sin × hiþin × bruþur × anutaʀ ×
uraiþr hik × runaʀ**

"Folkvid set up all these stones in memory of Heden, his son, Anund's
brother. Vred cut the runes."

Since it is beyond all doubt that the rune stone has always stood in the same
place, the phrase "all these stones" must refer to stones which are, or were, to be
found in the immediate vicinity of Heden's memorial. A good many years ago I
made a preliminary survey of the site and was then able to show that at least
thirteen of the stones were still there, sunk deep in the ground and hidden for
centuries. In the autumn of 1960 excavation of the area around the rune stone
was begun by staff of the State Department of Antiquities, and the work was
finished in the spring of 1961. We found fourteen of the original standing-stones
(*bautasteinar*), lying in a long, straight row. It is clear that Heden's memorial had
consisted of a roadway constructed on a truly grand scale: an avenue, flanked by a
long row of standing-stones, which had led from the river-ford on the northeast
to the Badelunda ridge on the southwest. The rune stone, taller than the
flankers, had stood at the centre of this stretch of roadway. It is of particular
interest that "all these stones" border *Eriksgata*, cf. p. 43 above. The complete
lay-out of the memorial now uncovered has been damaged by the removal of a
number of the standing-stones in connection with cultivation of the land round
the rune stone. Nevertheless, this may be justly called Sweden's proudest
"bridge" monument from the Viking Age. (On bridge-building see p. 106 f.
above.)

The good man

A man's distinction as sailor, warrior or public benefactor was not the only subject of eulogy in the runic inscriptions. Qualities such as generosity, benevolence and eloquence also find record in runic epitaphs.

The memorial of the dead brothers in the Turinge inscription (p. 58 f. above) includes the statement, "they maintained their household men well". Generosity was a characteristic of the chieftain, often praised in the ancient poetry. The little runic stanza on the Turinge stone expresses the same thoughts as are found, for example, in *Beowulf*, when in the last scene of the Anglo-Saxon epic the retainers stand lamenting round the burial mound of the hero. Beowulf's "hearth-companions" laud him as *manna mildust* "the most munificent of men", *leodum*

The men whose names are recorded on the Badelunda stone in Västmanland belonged to the greatest family in the neighbourhood.

liðost "the kindest to his people", and "keenest for fame"—*lofgeornost*.

An Uppland rune stone at Väppeby in Veckholm parish praises the dead man as · **mantr · matar · koþr · auk · mls · risia** *mandr mataʀ goðr ok malsrisinn* "a man generous with food and eloquent". On the Gådi stone (Uppland) Holmbjörn sings his own praises as **miltr · mataʀ · auk · mals · risin** "liberal with food and eloquent".

The same qualities are celebrated on the stone at Hagstugan (Södermanland), set up by four sons in memory of their good father, Domare: **: at : tumara : miltan : urþa uk : mataʀ kuþan :** *at Domara, mildan orða ok mataʀ goðan*. Precisely the same expression—*mildan orða ok mataʀ goðan*—is used of a dead father on the Ryssby stone (Småland).

A housewife who had run the estate while her husband was on Viking expeditions receives her homage in the inscription on the Hassmyra stone from Västmanland.

The nickname *inn malspaki* "the word-wise, eloquent" may also be mentioned. It is found on the Gillberga stone (Uppland), raised by sons in memory of **kara : faþur : sin : in : mal : sbaka : .**

A rune stone at Krageholm in Sövestad parish in Skåne ends its inscription with these words of praise: *hann var bæztr bomanna ok mildastr matar* "he was the best of yeomen and freest with food". The same liberality is given prominence in a stanza, unfortunately defective, on the Ivla stone (Småland). The stone was put up by Vimund in memory of his brother, Sven:

> *mildan við sinna*
> *ok matar góðan,*
> *i orðlofi*
> *allra miklu*

—"gentle towards his people / and generous with food, / in great esteem / with everyone". The old poem *Hávamál* provides close parallels to the expressions found on the rune stones:

> *Fannka ek mildan mann*
> *eða svá matar góðan...*

"I did not find so free a man / or one with food so liberal..."

The noun *oniðingʀ*, literally "un-dastard", is used in a number of verse inscriptions to denote an outstanding and munificent man. The Transjö stone (Småland) says:

> *Hann vaʀ manna*
> *mestr oniðingʀ.*
> *Eʀ a Ænglandi*
> *aldri tynði*

"He was among men / the most 'un-dastard'. / He in England / lost his life." That generosity was a highly-prized feature of character is suggested too by the name *Osnikinn* which appears in some inscriptions; it originally meant "the un-greedy".

In the busy times of sowing and harvest a farmer might well find himself abroad in Russia, Greece, Saxland or England, or stuck in a ship on the North Sea or the Black Sea. The responsibility of running the farm in his absence rested then on the shoulders of his wife. A Swedish housewife receives her homage on the Hassmyra stone (Västmanland), set up by "the good yeoman", Holmgöt of Hassmyra, in memory of Odindisa, his wife:

buonti ✕ kuþr ✕ hulmkoetr ✕ lit✕ resa ✕ ufteʀ ✕ oþintisu ✕ kunu ✕ seno ✕ kumbr ✕

hifrya × til × hasuimura × iki betr × þon × byi raþr roþbalir × risti × runi × þisa × sik-
muntaʀ × aʀ [× oþintisa ×] sestʀ × kuþ

Boandi goðr Holmgautr let ræisa æftiʀ Oðindisu, kunu sina.

> *Kumbʀ hifrøya*
> *til Hasvimyra*
> *æigi bætri,*
> *þan byi raðr.*
> *Rauð-Balliʀ risti*
> *runiʀ þessaʀ.*
> *Sigmundaʀ vaʀ Oðindisa*
> *systiʀ goð.*

"There will not come to Hassmyra a better mistress who holds sway over the farm. Balle the Red cut these runes. To Sigmund was Odindisa a good sister."

The pride taken by the widowed mistress of the house in the monument which she and her four sons raised in memory of Fot finds appealing expression in the verse which ends the inscription on the Härene stone in Västergötland:

Sva hæfiʀ Asa	"Åsa has wrought
es æigi mun	what no wife will
sum kvæn æft ver	ever afterward
siðan gærva.	in husband's memory.
Hialmʀ ok Hialli	Hjälm and Hjälle
hioggu runaʀ.	hewed the runes."

In conclusion, it is perhaps not out of the way to emphasise that the runic inscriptions, however strident and warlike they may be, are themselves representative of cultural and artistic endeavours. The inscriptions convey not only feelings of loss and grief but also give expression, eloquent and precious, to the artistic aspirations of the age. They are among the most outstanding examples of ancient Sweden's artistic creativity. The rune carvers often reveal themselves as veritable masters of their art, both in the visual effects they achieve with their adornment of the stone's variously shaped surfaces and in the literary composition of the epitaphs they inscribe. The inscriptions are memorial notices cut on cramped faces, and as such must inevitably be limited both in subject-matter and in extent. Nevertheless, it is possible to learn something from them of the capabilities of the language at that time, and with their help not a few conclusions concerning the early history of Swedish and Norse literature can be drawn. Despite all their limitations they can, for example, give us some insight into the poetry which attentive audiences once heard the ancient makers deliver.

over the strand of the Reid-sea". This is a name which also belongs to the poetic style. It means no more than the "land of the Reid-Goths", a tribal name frequently attested though of uncertain sense. The hero-king sits *a gota sinum*: *goti* is a word used in poetry for "horse". In the last line of the stanza he is called *skati Mæringa* "prince of the Mærings", and a parallel to this is found in the Old English *Deor,* where it says:

> *Þeodric ahte*
> *þritig wintra*
> *Mæringa burg:*
> *þæt was monegum cuþ.*

"Theodric held / for thirty winters / the Mærings' fortress: / that was known to many." There was probably no great lapse of time between the inscription of the Rök stone and the composition of the Anglo-Saxon poem.

On the whole, it may be said that the rune-stone verse of Sweden, both in form and diction, is completely at home in the literary milieu which we know so well from early Norwegian and Icelandic poetry. It is a happy chance that at least this one example of the poetry made in Götaland in the ninth century was recorded in runes and, thanks to the durability of the material on which it was inscribed, has been preserved to our time. And we should perhaps not forget to note that our record of this little Swedish poem is older by several centuries than our sources for the old poetry of Norway and Iceland, which, as will be well known, is mostly extant only in manuscripts from late medieval times.

As I mentioned earlier, the Rök inscription opens with some particularly impressive runes. The alliteration and ceremonious rhythm give an impression of highly-wrought artistic prose: *Aft Væmoð standa runaʀ þaʀ. En Varinn faði, faðiʀ, aft faigian sunu* "In memory of Væmod stand these runes. And Varin wrote them, the father, in memory of his dead son".

In the text itself are also many examples of phrasing and word-order characteristic of poetic style. A well-known type of kenning occurs, for instance, in the sentence, with its calculated rhythmical effects, which immediately follows the Theodric stanza: *Þat sagum tvalfta, hvar hæstʀ se Gunnaʀ etu vettvangi an, kunungaʀ tvaiʀ tigiʀ svað a liggia* "That I tell twelfth where the horse of Gunn [= the horse of the Valkyrie, the wolf] sees food on the battlefield, where twenty kings lie".

The Rök stone is of course a unique literary monument but, as we have seen, the rune stones of the eleventh century also offer many specimens of poetry, albeit of a more ordinary kind and easier to understand.

In this connection our interest will naturally be attracted by the signature of the rune carver at the end of the long inscription on the Hillersjö rock (p. 97 f.

132

above): *Þorbiorn skald*. He is not the only rune-master to give himself the cognomen *skald* "scald, poet"—we know a *Grimr skald* in Uppland and an *Uddr skald* in Västergötland. We wish we knew what the poetry was like which gained this honourable title for Torbjörn, Grim and Udd.

We should remember that the word *skald* by no means had the specialised sense which modern literary historians give to the terms "scald", "scaldic poetry" and "scaldic poem"—this specialised reference is sometimes conveyed by terms like English "court-poet", "court-poetry". The adjective "scaldic" is a modern technical term generally used to denote types of Norse poetry which, in part because of their more intricate artistry, stand in some contrast to the simpler, more popular, and anonymous eddaic poems. This restricted sense of the word *skald* did not of course exist when the rune stones were inscribed. The word meant "poet" and gave no indication of what kind of verse a man composed. Thus, the appearance of the word in runic inscriptions is not in itself evidence that scaldic poets, in the technical sense of the term, flourished in Sweden, although there are other good grounds for believing that they did.

It is indeed evident that in their time Swedish audiences also strained respectful ears to catch the full import of the highly-wrought diction of scaldic poetry, with its involute kennings and images often rich and intricate, its strict metrical rules governing the number of syllables to the line and the obligatory alliteration and assonance. For we know that many practitioners of this characteristic Norse art-poetry visited Sweden, where they recited their poems in the presence of kings and noblemen. Icelandic tradition says that Brage the Old, the first scald, visited King Björn in Birka and made a poem in his honour—that would be at about the same time as St Ansgar visited King Björn on a different errand. Óttarr the Black made poetry in praise of King Olav the Swede (died *c.* 1020) and, according to Snorri, Hjalti Skeggjason and Gizurr the Black also visited his court. Other Icelandic poets who are said to have come to this Swedish king are Hallfreðr the Troublesome Poet, Hrafn Önundarson and Gunnlaugr Snake-Tongue, while Olav's son, King Anund Jakob, was eulogised by Sighvatr Þórðarson and Óttarr the Black. Visits from Icelandic court-poets continued for a surprisingly long time: Sturla Þórðarson, Snorri Sturluson's nephew, was able to compose a poem in honour of Birger Jarl (died 1266) before this aristocratic and traditional formalistic poetry finally lost all its public appeal.

The inscription on the copper box from Sigtuna, described on p. 56 above, includes a couplet in the favoured scaldic metre called *dróttkvætt*. The lines may be rendered thus:

> *Fugl velva slæit falvan,*
> *fann'k gauk a nas auka*

"The bird tore the pale thief. I saw how the corpse-cuckoo swelled".

The word *velva* (acc.) is probably the same as Gothic *wilwa* m. "robber". The phrase *nas gaukr* "corpse's cuckoo" is a kenning for the raven, chief of "carrion-crows". Comparable expressions are found in Icelandic scaldic verse, e.g. *hræva gaukr* "carrion's cuckoo". That the raven should gorge on the corpse of the thief is an idea completely in harmony with the poetic imagery we met on the Gripsholm stone (p. 64 f. above) and on the Rök stone, where the "horse of the Valkyrie" was gladdened by the dead bodies on the battlefield.

A fact that deserves notice is that the only complete *dróttkvætt* stanza of which we possess the original text—i.e. one recorded in the Viking Age itself—is to be found on Swedish territory. This is the strophe which forms the last part of the inscription on the Karlevi stone (Öland). The stone was set up about the year 1000 in memory of a chieftain, Sibbe Foldar's son, who was buried on the west coast of the island. The stanza reads: **fulkin : likr : hins : fulkþu : flaistr : uisi : þat · maistar · taiþir : tulka þruþar : traukr : i : þaimsi · huki : munat : raiþ : uiþur : raþa : ruk : starkr i : tanmarku : ạintils : iarmun · kruntar : urkrạntari : lạnti.** Or put into an Old Icelandic form:

> *Fólginn liggr, hinns fylgðu*
> *(flestr vissi þat) mestar*
> *dæðir, dólga Þrúðar*
> *draugr, í þeimsi haugi.*
> *Munat reið-Viðurr ráða*
> *rógstarkr í Danmǫrku*
> *Endils iǫrmungrundar*
> *ørgrandari landi.*

A relatively literal version gives the following not entirely perspicuous text in English: "Hidden lies the man whom the greatest virtues accompanied—most men knew that—executor of the goddess of battles—in this mound. A more honest battle-strong god of the wagon of the mighty ground of the sea-king will not rule over land in Denmark."

The Karlevi strophe complies with all the strict rules of *dróttkvætt* and makes the classic demands of this metre and style on the reader's familiarity with the tradition and his literary alertness. (The term *dróttkvætt, dróttkvæðr háttr* means, we recall, the "metre suitable for verse made for delivery before the court of a king or chieftain". The word *drótt* f. is an old collective for the sworn retainers, the picked warriors, of a leader, the later *hirðmenn*. Cf. Runic Swedish **trutin**, OSw. *drotin*, ON *dróttinn* "lord"; OSw. *drotseti*, ON *dróttseti* "marshal".) We see that the Karlevi stanza has the regular eight lines composed in two quatrains, each line with three stressed syllables, internal half-rhyme (*skothending*) and full rhyme (*aðalhending*) in alternate lines, and impeccable alliteration.

Imagery and phrasing throughout are also typical of scaldic style. The very first word—*folginn*—has interesting correspondences in West Norse poetry. It is

The Karlevi stone on Öland is the only rune stone in the world with a complete *dróttkvætt* stanza on it.

the past part. of the strong verb *fela* "hide, conceal", which in *Ynglingatal* is used to mean "bury": ... *ok buðlung / á Borrói / sigrhafendr / síðan fálu* "and those with the victory afterwards buried the king at Borre". The chieftain buried at Karlevi is then called *dólga Þrúðar draugr*. The last word, *draugr* m., is often used in kennings for "warrior"; *dólga draugr* would be the "doer, performer of battles".

The word *draugr* appears to be a nomen agentis from the strong verb *driuga* (Gothic *driugan*) "struggle, accomplish; do, perform (work of some kind)". It is worth noting that this verb, which fell out of use early in the Nordic languages, is attested in the pret. sg. in the verse of the eleventh-century Fagerlöt inscription (Södermanland): *Hann draug*—**trauh**—*orrustu i austrvegi* "He did battle on the eastern route". See p. 140.

The two other words in the kenning referring to the dead leader, *dólga Þrúðar*, are also well known in eddaic and scaldic verse. *Dólg* n. means "hostility, strife, battle", cf. *dólga dynr* in *Helgakviða Hundingsbana I*, "din of battle(s)". *Þrúðr* is the name of a goddess, said to be a daughter of Thor—he is referred to as *faðir Þrúðar*.

The whole expression *dólga Þrúðar draugr* consequently means something like "executor, performer of the goddess of battles", i.e. warrior or war-lord.

Another periphrasis for "leader, chieftain" is found in the words *Endils iǫrmungrundar reið-Viðurr*. *Endill* is the name of a sea-king, *iǫrmungrund* means "mighty ground, vast expanse"—a sea-king's "mighty ground" is simply a kenning for "sea". The compound *reið-Viðurr* means "wagon- (or chariot-) Vidur"—*Viðurr* is one of Odin's many names. The "wagon" one uses on the sea is a ship, and the Odin or god of the ship is her powerful commander.

The word *iǫrmungrund* in the Karlevi kenning **aintils : larmun · kruntar : raiþ : uiþur** is also found for example in *Beowulf*—*eormengrund*—and in the eddaic poem, *Grímnismál*, where it says: *Huginn ok Muninn / fliúga hverian dag / iǫrmungrund yfir*—"Huginn and Muninn [Odin's ravens] fly each day over earth's wide surface". The word thus suggests a homogeneity in the early poetic language, not confined to the Norse area.

A number of inscriptions in verse have been quoted above to illustrate various aspects of life in ancient Sweden. A translation of the inscription on the Bällsta stones was cited, for instance, in connection with the discussion of assembly places (p. 121 above). The fourteen lines of verse there offer much of interest but I shall only pause to consider the last pair:

> *Þy man i grati*
> *getit lata.*

The Icelandic scholar, Jón Helgason, has suggested that the words *i grati*, literally "in weeping", should be interpreted as meaning "in a lament"—cf. the titles of poems like *Oddrúnargrátr, Máríugrátr*, "the weeping of Oddrún", "the weeping of Mary". In this there would be support for the assumption, in itself not unnatural, that laments or dirges, related in kind to the West Norse *Eiríksmál* and Egill Skalla-Grímsson's *Sonatorrek*, were also composed in Sweden in the Viking Age. One must however hasten to add that we should be presuming too far if we thought that Ulv's wife and sons could command the service of Swedish poets comparable in genius to the creators of these two West Norse masterpieces. Nevertheless, we would give much to know just how this postulated *gratr* sounded, this unrecorded song of lament that was to keep Ulv's memory alive. But we must rest content with the simpler runes inscribed to his memory that are still to be read on the stone.

These last words at Bällsta, *Py man i grati / getit lata*, are paralleled in some degree by lines on the Nöbbele stone (Småland): *Py mun goðs mans / um getit verða* "Therefore the noble man shall be spoken of". But this entire inscription is in verse and deserves quotation as a whole:

Hroðstæinn ok Æilifʀ,	"Rodsten and Eliv,
Aki ok Hakon	Åke and Håkon,
ræistu þæiʀ svæinaʀ	those lads raised
æftiʀ sinn faður	after their father
kumbl kænniligt,	an eye-catching 'kuml',
æftiʀ Kala dauðan.	after Kale dead.
Py mun goðs mans	So of the noble man
um getit verða,	shall mention be made
með stæinn lifiʀ	as long as stone lives
ok stafiʀ runa.	and letters of runes."

A whole strophe in *fornyrðislag* is found on an earth-embedded rock inscribed with runes at Fyrby (Södermanland):

Iak væit Hastæin,	"I know Håsten
þa Holmstæin brøðr,	and Holmsten, brothers,
mænnr rynasta	to be the most rune-skilled men
a Miðgarði.	in Middlegarth.
Sættu stæin	They placed stone
ok stafa marga	and many staves
æftiʀ Frøystæin,	after Frösten
faður sinn.	their father."

The Fyrby inscription from Södermanland tells of the custom of placing "stone and staves" as a memorial.

With every sign of self-confidence, the brothers describe themselves as *mænnr rynasta a Miðgarði*. As we know, the term *Miðgarðr* "the middle world"— i.e. the home of mankind, protected by the gods—is a highflown expression, familiar from other Germanic languages besides Norse—Gothic *midjungards*, OHG *mittingart*, OE *middangeard*.—The adj. *rynn* "rune-skilled" also occurs in the stanza on the Ågersta stone (p. 97 above) and in a runic inscription in Orkney. In this third instance (Maeshowe 18) the carver merely takes credit for being the most rune-skilled man "west over the sea":

> *Þessar rúnar*
> *reist sá maðr,*
> *er rýnstr er*
> *fyrir vestan haf...*

He is too modest to claim that he is *rýnstr á Miðgarði*.

Another inscription composed in verse throughout, like that on the Nöbbele stone, was on the rune stone at Hagstugan (Södermanland), but the end of it is now damaged:

> fiuriʀ : kirþu :   *Fiuriʀ gærðu*
> at : faþur : kuþan :   *at faður góðan*

tyrþ : trikela	*dyrð drængila*
: at : tumara :	*at Domara,*
miltan : urþa	*mildan orða*
uk : mataʀ kuþan : ...	*ok mataʀ goðan ...*

"Four sons made / for noble father / manly a memorial, / for Domare, / gentle in word / and generous with food..."

The rune sequence **tyrþ** can hardly represent anything but *dyrð* f., ON *dýrð* "splendour, glory". The word occurs nowhere else in Runic or early Swedish. In the seventeenth century it was borrowed for purist reasons (Stiernhielm) and *dyrd* was then used by a number of later authors, Viktor Rydberg and Karlfeldt among them. It is difficult to say what the precise sense of the word in the Hagstugan inscription is, but it seems likely that it was intended to refer to the rune stone itself: in its fresh state it would appear a sufficient splendour. (We may note too that the verse-maker needed a word that would alliterate with *Domari*.)

The inscription on the rune stones at Tjuvstigen (*þiuðstigr?* "public path") in Södermanland consists of twelve lines, making three half-strophes in *fornyrð-islag:*

Styrlaugʀ ok Holmʀ	"Styrlög and Holm
stæina ræistu	raised the stones
at brøðr sina	after their brothers
brautu næsta.	next to the road.
Þæiʀ ændaðus	They met their end
i austrvegi,	on the eastern route,
Þorkell ok Styrbiorn,	Thorkel and Styrbjörn,
þiagnaʀ goðiʀ.	noble 'thegns'.
Let Ingigærðr	Ingigärd let raise
annan ræisa stæin	another stone
at syni sina,	after her sons,
syna gærði.	a visible cenotaph."

The Tjuvstigen stones were thus set up by the mother and brothers of the lost eastern voyagers *brautu næsta* "next to the road". A closely similar expression is used by Balle on the Ryda stone (Uppland), set up beside the main road that leads to the royal estate there:

Her mun standa	"Here shall stand
stæinn næʀ brautu.	the stone near the road."

Reading these inscriptions and seeing rune stones by the wayside bring readily to mind the words of *Hávamál:*

Sialdan bautarsteinar
standa brautu nær,
nema reisi niðr at nið.

"Seldom *bauta*-stones stand near the road, if kinsman does not raise them after kinsman." These same lines are also called to mind by the inscriptions on two rune stones in Småland, at Bräkentorp and Skaftarp, in both of which we are told that the memorial—*vitring þessa*—stands "at the road-junction"—*a vægamoti*.

In speaking of journeys to *Langbarðaland* (p. 73 above), I cited the Djulefors quatrain, whose lines of intricate artistry tell us that the dead man *austarla arði barði ok a Langbarða landi andaðis.* The figurative "plough with the ship's prow" is found in an anonymous Icelandic fragment: *Sá's af Íslandi / arði barði* "He who from Iceland / ploughed with the prow"; and Rögnvaldr Kolsson, twelfth-century earl of Orkney, uses the same image as the rune-carver of Södermanland: *Erjum úrgu barði / út at Miklagarði* "Let us plough with wet prow / out to Micklegard".

Parallels to West Norse poetry can also be found on the Fagerlöt block (Södermanland). It has the interesting expressions, *driuga orrostu* (cf.p. 136 above) and *folks grimR*, "do battle" and "chieftain":

Hann draug orrostu	"He did battle
i austrvegi	on the eastern route
aðan folks grimR	before the host-chief
falla orði.	fell perforce."

As we have seen from the passages and parallels quoted earlier, this kind of correspondence is by no means a rarity.

Reading some Swedish inscriptions we now and then have the feeling that we have stumbled on fragments, "quotations", from larger poems that are otherwise completely lost. Perhaps the best example of this is offered by the Skarpåker stone (Södermanland). After the introduction, "Gunnar raised this stone in memory of Lydbjörn, his son", come two lines in *fornyrðislag,* cut in the staveless runes that were developed for practical everyday notation (see pp. 28 f., 100 above). The lines read:

Iarð skal rifna	"Earth shall be riven
ok upphiminn.	and the over-heaven."

(We may note that the alliteration here is in full accord with the metrical rules: an initial *i*-sound like that in *iarð* (now written *j* in the Scandinavian languages and pronounced like English *y*) should alliterate with a vowel, preferably one of different quality, as in *upphiminn.*)

It is tempting to regard these stray lines on the Skarpåker stone as a quotation from a Swedish poem on the "doom of the gods" (ON *ragnarǫk*), so well known at the time the inscription was written that everyone would understand their message—a poem which a father's grief found fitting to call to mind by these two allusive lines.

The antithetic word-pair, *iarð—upphiminn*, is well attested in other Germanic poetry. We find them in the *Vǫluspá's* famous lines on the creation of the world:

Vara sandr né sær,	"There was no sand, no sea,
né svalar unnir.	no surges cold.
iǫrð fannz æva,	There was no earth
né upphiminn.	nor over-heaven;
Gap var ginnunga,	a gaping void was all,
en gras hvergi.	but grass nowhere."

The words occur elsewhere in the *Edda*. In *Vafþrúðnismál* Odin asks the all-wise giant:

hvaðan iǫrð um kom	"Whence came the earth
eða upphiminn	or the over-heaven
fyrst, inn fróði iǫtunn?	first, O giant full of lore?"

In *Þrymskviða* Thor breaks the disturbing news of the theft of his hammer:

"Heyrðu nú, Loki,	"Attend now, Loke,
hvat ek nú mæli,	to what I now tell,
er eigi veit	which no one knows
iarðar hvergi	anywhere on earth
né upphimins:	nor in over-heaven:
áss er stolinn hamri!"	the god is robbed of his hammer!"

And finally we read in *Oddrúnargrátr*:

Iǫrð dúsaði	"The earth resounded
ok upphiminn,	and the over-heaven
þá er bani Fáfnis	when Fafner's slayer
borg um þátti.	espied the fortress."

A recently discovered inscription contains the same pair of words. A little wooden stick, found during excavations at Ribe in Denmark, has a runic charm against sickness (malaria) on it. The inscription, of interest from many points of view, begins with a *fornyrðislag* strophe, whose first lines read:

Iorþ biþ ak uarþæ	"Earth I pray ward
ok uphimæn . . .	and over-heaven . . ."

This Ribe inscription is probably from the thirteenth century, but charms of this type have very ancient roots. The same formula is found, for example, in an Anglo-Saxon charm from the eighth century:

> *eorðan ic bidde*
> *and upheofon . . .*

In conveying the cataclysmic atmosphere of the doom of the gods, the poet of *Vǫluspá* at one point uses words that bear a certain resemblance to the image in the Skarpåker inscription of the rending of earth and heaven:

Grjóthjǫrg gnata	"Rock-cliffs crash
— — — — —	— — — — —
en himinn klofnar.	and heaven is cleft."

(On a picture portraying the last battle between the gods and the giants, see p. 152 below.)

Other stanzas that might well be thought to contain "quotations" of this kind are those on the Rök stone and the Gripsholm stone (pp. 32, 65 above).

In the porch of the church at Vallentuna there is now a rune stone which has an inscription of great interest for the history of literature. It ends with these three lines of verse:

Hann drunknaði a Holms hafi.	"He drowned in the Holm's sea.
Skræið knarr hans i kaf,	His ship sank bodily,
þriʀ æiniʀ kvamo af.	those who lived were only three."

It is the *verse form* which is especially noteworthy. It is unique among runic verse of the Viking Age by reason of its end-rhyme. It represents the oldest known Swedish example of this novel metrical feature, which in the middle ages was to become the general rule. End-rhyme and imported metres were to replace alliteration as the basic and binding element in Swedish verse. Alliteration was indeed ousted throughout the Germanic world, although it lived till late in the middle ages in parts of England and has never died out in Iceland, where men keep faith with their traditions. Our rune-writers' age-old convention of *forn-yrðislag* was superseded by the loose octosyllabic couplets of rhymed *knittelvers* and the pliant forms of the ballad. Here it is interesting to note that the poet of the Vallentuna verse used both modes—alliteration *and* end-rhyme.

In itself, after all, there is nothing surprising in the appearance of end-rhyme in a verse from the end of the eleventh century. Nearly two hundred years earlier, ringing rhyme had been produced in sensational circumstances in the hall of King Erik Blood-axe in York, when Egill Skalla-Grímsson "bore Odin's mead over the Angles' land". But the three lines of the Uppland inscription show the first known Swedish attempt to make use of this up-to-date continental verse form. End-rhyme occurs later in runic verses on gravestones, but runic memorials of that kind belong not to the Viking Age but to the medieval culture of the Swedes.

Many of the runic strophes cited above form part of inscriptions which have been *signed* by the rune-masters. This is a remarkable fact, not least because we otherwise have to wait several centuries before any pieces of Swedish writing emerge from the darkness of anonymity. Indeed, right down to the middle of the fifteenth century all other Swedish literature in the vernacular is anonymous.

Both alliteration and end-rhyme are used in the verse in the inscription on this stone, now in Vallentuna church.

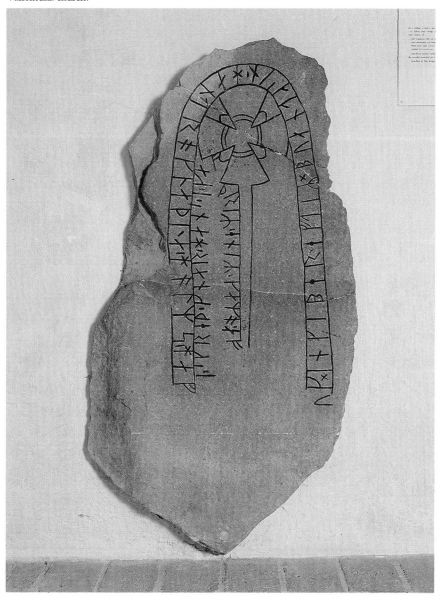

Pictures on rune stones

The rune-writers are not only Sweden's first known authors—they are also our oldest named artists. The inscriptions of the rune-masters are not exclusively sources of linguistic, literary and historical interest: their work may also justly claim a place in the history of Swedish art.

Rune carvers like Åsmund Kåresson, Äskil, Fot, Livsten, Balle the Red and Öpir, created and developed the Swedish rune-stone style. Their art is essentially decorative; their feeling for proportion and linear rhythm is often superb. Their art-form—which in its restless and constant movement seems to be an expression of their own times—represents the last offshoot from the animal ornament of the early Germanic peoples. Pictorial representation does occur on a number of stones (see below), but for the most part these belong to monuments of a different order—the picture stones of Gotland.

These Gotland monuments of pictorial art, whose golden age lay as far back as the eighth century, give us rich and living illustrations of myths, legends and poems—most of which are unfortunately totally unknown to us. The subject-matter of the picture series on any given stone—certainly entirely intelligible to the age that created them—is hidden from us in an almost impenetrable obscurity. We have the illustrations but not the captions. (This applies equally of course to pictorial scenes on other ancient objects, in metal for example—from the golden horns of Gallehus onwards.)

From the point of view of art history the Gotland picture stones are of extraordinary interest. With their innumerable figures, their warlike men and proud horses, their ships sailing under lozenge-patterned sails over turbulent seas, they give us a unique glimpse into the picture world of the ancients. But they usually have no runic inscriptions on them, and they are very different in character from the common kind of rune stone—though it is true that the famous Ardre stones, in both ornament and runic inscriptions, stand on the borderline between the two types. Place cannot be found for the Gotland stones in the present account; they deserve a chapter of their own.

As mentioned above, however, pictures are not entirely lacking on the ordinary rune stones, although they are usually in a purely decorative style.

To judge from the pictures on Swedish rune stones, by far the most popular hero of legend was Sigurd, the slayer of Favner the dragon. He is a figure

144

introduced in several carvings but his story is depicted in most detail and best executed on the famous rock at Ramsund in Södermanland, not far from Eskilstuna. Some of the most dramatic episodes in the hero's career are reproduced there—not in words, for the runic text is a "bridge" inscription of the usual kind, but in pictures. We see Sigurd in his pit, using enormous force to thrust his broad sword, forged by Regin, through the massive trunk of the dragon's body—this forms the band in which the runes are inscribed. At the left end of the carved surface lies the body of the treacherous Regin with his head cut off, and immediately to the right of him we see the smithy, with its bellows, hammer, anvil and tongs. Sigurd sits there and roasts Favner's heart over the smithy fire. He has just burnt himself, trying the dragon's heart to see if it is properly cooked, and has stuck his scorched thumb into his mouth to ease the pain: "But when the dragon's heart's blood came on his tongue, he understood the language of birds. He heard the marsh-tits twittering...", as it says in the prose accompanying the eddaic poem *Fáfnismál*.

Þar sitr Sigurðr,	"There sits Sigurd
sveita stokkinn,	spattered with blood,
Fáfnis hiarta	Favner's heart
við funa steikir.	he broils at the fire.
Spakr þœtti mér	Wise would seem to me
spillir bauga,	the spoiler of rings
ef hann fiǫrsega	if he were to eat
fránan æti.	the shining life-muscle."

The marsh-tits who warn Sigurd are also pictured on the Ramsund rock; they sit in a handsomely stylised tree, to which Grane, Sigurd's horse, is also tethered.

The rune-stone pictures of Gunnar in the snake-pen, another of the great moments of climax in the Völsung story, also introduce us to the literary background of ancient Scandinavia. The hero appears in several pictures, not only on stones, wreathed about with snakes and trying to defend himself against them. The theme was undeniably well suited to artists of the Viking Age, who had a deep-rooted love for patterns of entwining serpents. The Västerljung stone (Södermanland) is carved on three sides. On one of them a recently discovered picture shows a man with his arms and one of his legs trapped by twining snakes. He holds his arms stretched out in front of him and has a large object in his hand. It is at least possible that the object is a harp, but the surface of the stone has flaked near the edge of the stone where it was carved and the lines of it severely damaged. If this does represent Gunnar in the snake-pen, we can say that he is not playing his harp with his toes—which is the version found in

Above: The pictures of the Ramsundsberget carving shows episodes from the legend of Sigurd, the slayer of Fafner the dragon. *Below:* Left. Sigurd thrusting his sword through the dragon's body. Right. Sigurd roasting the dragon's heart over the smithy fire.

Atlamál (and from there in *Völsunga saga*) and on the Norum font (see p. 170 below), as well as in a number of scenes on Norwegian stave-churches. He is playing it with his fingers, in the same way as in the archaic eddaic poem, *Atlakviða*. Besides being the most practical method, this is almost certainly the original form of the motif in the legend of Gunnar's death. As far as that goes, it seems likely in any case that the harp was introduced comparatively late into the

The legend of Sigurd is also the motif on the Drävle stone from Uppland.

story. At least, the carving on the Oseberg cart shows Gunnar defending himself without the aid of any instrument—and that carving can be dated to the mid-ninth century, some 200 years before the Västerljung stone was inscribed. It is also worth noting that here Gunnar—if Gunnar it is—sits on a chair in the snake-pen. That seems a feature which is too idyllic—too much in keeping with a cosy Södermanland outlook—to be suitable for the pathos and high heroism of the Völsung epic—which hardly has room for creature comforts.

The moving, grim story of Völund the master-smith was also known, as we see from the pictures on one of the Ardre stones (Gotland). There we make out his smithy with hammer and tongs, the headless bodies of King Nidud's young sons, Bödvild, the ravished princess, and Völund's bird-shape.

These figures are familiar to us primarily from the eddaic poem, *Vǫlundar-kviða*. As we recall, it describes how Völund sits solitary in Wolf-dales, vainly waiting for the return of the mysterious swan-maiden who had once put her arms round his neck and lived with him as his wife. He is suddenly attacked and captured by King Nidud, who forces him to make treasures for him—to prevent his escape the king has his knee-tendons severed. In revenge Völund kills the two young sons of Nidud and makes jewels from their skulls, eyes and teeth for the royal family; then he rapes the king's daughter, Bödvild, who trustingly brings him a gold ring for repair. Finally Völund flies away from his captivity with the help of wings which he seems to have made in secret—a Germanic Daedalus, hovering inaccessible among the clouds.

That this was a favoured theme in the early English world is evident, among other things, from the fascinating and famous whalebone box called the Franks Casket. One of the front panels has dramatic scenes from Völund's career carved on it. The pictures on this side of the box are framed by alliterating verse cut in runes, though their subject-matter bears no direct relation to the illustrations. The casket was probably made at the end of the seventh century.

Left: This picture of one of the sides of the Västerljung stone probably shows Gunnar in the snake-pen playing the harp. *Right:* The font at Norum in Bohuslän was made in the early twelfth century. Below the runes there is a picture of Gunnar in the snake-pen playing the harp with his feet.

If Sigurd the slayer of Favner was one of the most admired heroes of ancient legend, it was evidently Thor and his adventures that were the most popular of all the gods and myths. His fight with the "World Serpent" was a theme particularly favoured by poets and artists. One of the pictures on the rune stone

The stone from Ardre on Gotland stands on the borderline between the two types of stones that were erected, picture stones and runic stones.

at Altuna church (Uppland), carved by "Balle and Frösten, Livsten's team"—
Balli, Frøystæinn, lið Lifstæin[s ristu]—must be an illustration of the old tale of
Thor's great expedition to fish for the Midgarth Serpent. The stone was set up in
memory of father and son, Holmfast and Arnfast, who "were both burnt in their
house".

On the lower part of this side of the stone there is a picture of a man standing
in a boat which has a very high stem and stern and a massive rudder. The man in
the boat stands face-on to the spectator. In his right hand he has a lifted hammer,
while from his left a very thick rope runs down into the water. At the other end

Left: One of the pictures on the rune stone at Altuna church in Uppland must be an illustration of
the old tale of Thor's great expedition to fish for the Midgarth Serpent. *Right:* This witch-woman
riding a wolf and using a snake for reins is on one of the Hunnestad stones in Skåne.

of the rope hangs a clumsy-looking object, which must certainly be intended to represent a piece of bait of unusual size. Below and beside the bait a sea-monster is coiled. There can be no doubt but that the man in the boat is Thor, the hammer is Mjölner, the bait is the ox-head, which Thor wrenched off one of the giant Hymer's beasts, and the monster is the "World Serpent". The agreement between the picture on the Altuna stone and the description of this episode in West Norse literary sources is very close. The story told by Snorri Sturluson in his *Edda* (*c.* 1220) may serve as an explanatory text to the Uppland rune-stone picture carved some two centuries earlier: "The Midgarth Serpent bit at the ox-head and the hook caught in the roof of its mouth. When it felt that, it started so violently that both Thor's fists went smack against the gunwale. Then Thor got

The scene depicted on the Ledberg stone from Östergötland is probaly from the Ragnarök drama.

151

angry, assumed all his godly strength, and dug in his heels so sturdily that his feet went right through the bottom of the boat and he braced them on the sea-bed." The drastic detail about Thor's legs, shoved through the ship's bottom as a result of his enormous exertion, is not omitted on the rune stone. We see there how Thor's left leg is driven halfway through the planks.

There is evidence to suggest that the scene depicted on the splendid Ledberg stone (Östergötland), with its carvings on three sides, is from the Ragnarök drama. At the top of one side a huge helmeted warrior can be seen. Below the warrior a beast is tearing at his foot. The beast is probably the Wolf Fenrer, the brother of the Midgarth Serpent, and in that case the warrior attacked by the fearsome quadruped must be Odin. The bottom figure on the stone is that of a half-prostrate helmeted man. He has no legs and his arms are held out feebly in front of him. A striking parallel to the Ledberg picture is found on a tenth-century stone cross at Kirk Andreas in the Isle of Man: Odin, armed with a spear and with one of his ravens on his shoulder, is being attacked there in exactly the same way by the monstrous wolf. (We may note too that the Ledberg inscription ends with an interesting magic formula which is known from all over the ancient Norse world.)

There are other pictures that can lead our thoughts into the realm of early myth and poetry. Thus, on one of the Hunnestad stones (Skåne) we see a witch-woman riding on an animal—undoubtedly meant to be a wolf—and using a snake for reins. This might serve as an illustration to accompany the description of *Hyrrokin*, "the fire-wrinkled", when the gods summoned her from the world of giants to launch Baldr's ship, *Hringhorni*, too heavy for them to move: "And when she came, she rode on a wolf and had a snake for reins" (*En er hon kom ok reið vargi ok hafði hǫggorm at taumum*), as it says in Snorri's *Edda*. It was a wolf like this, moreover, which the Rök inscription refers to as "the Valkyrie's horse", who spies food on the battle-field where twenty kings lie.

Sometimes more everyday scenes are depicted on the rune stones. The rune carver of the Böksta stone (Uppland) has given us a picture from an elk-hunt in winter (see p. 154). The stone has been damaged, but the subject of the illustration is quite clear. In the middle of the carved face there is a horseman with a spear in his hand, and in front of him two dogs give chase to an elk; at the extreme left a man is standing on skis, ready to let fly his arrow at the fugitive game. A large bird is depicted at the top, and another bird has struck his talons into the elk's head. If the whole simply represents a hunting scene, then these birds must be decorative hawks, birds trained for falconry.

COLOUR

In this very brief discussion of pictorial and decorative elements on rune stones, it is not inappropriate to recall that the inscriptions were originally painted in different colours. The use of colour must have meant a remarkable addition to the beauty and artistic effect of the monuments. Painting also served a practical purpose, for without colour the runes themselves would in most cases have been all too difficult to pick out and the often intricate ornament difficult to follow. Once upon a time, then, the runes, the decorative motifs, and the pictures all shone in bright colours. That this is historical fact and not an assumption based on any *a priori* notions about the Vikings' love of rich colour has been most strikingly demonstrated by recent runic discoveries. Some rune stones, moreover, tell us themselves that they were painted.

Of particular interest in this connection is the stanza on one of the stones at Överselö church (Södermanland): **: hir : skal : stenta : staena : þisiʀ : runum : ru[þ]niʀ : ·· raisti : k[uþl]auk : at syni : sina : auk : hielmlauk : at bryþr : sina ·**

Her skal standa	"Here shall stand
stæinaʀ þessiʀ,	these stones,
runum ruðniʀ,	red with runes,
ræisti Guðlaug	Gudlög raised them
at syni sina,	after her sons
ok Hialmlaug	and Hjälmlög
at brøðr sina.	after her brothers."

The phrase *stæinaʀ, runum ruðniʀ,* may be compared with the words, *stafir, ristnir ok roðnir,* in the eddaic poem, *Guðrúnarkviða II*:

Vóru í horni	"There were in the horn
hvers kyns stafir	all kinds of rune-letters
ristnir ok roðnir—	cut and red-coloured—
ráða ek né máttak...	read them I could not..."

Thus according to the rune-writer's own account the Överselö stones were "reddened with runes"— reddened as far as the runes were concerned. This construction with the dat.—*runum ruðniʀ*—is usual in the old language. The word *ruðniʀ* is nom. pl. masc. of the past part. of *riuða* (ON *rjóða*) "to redden". The alliterative *riuða odd ok egg* "redden point and edge" (of a weapon, with blood) is found in OSw. (and Old West Norse) law-language. In the manslaughter section of *Yngre Västgötalagen* it says: *þu røt hanum oð ok æg. ok þu æst sander bani hans* "you reddened point and edge on him and you are his true slayer". In the immunities section of *Upplandslagen* it says that an oath swearing misadventure is necessary *at rinnændæ bloþi ok riuþændæ sari* "at running blood and reddening wound".

The Överselö inscription gives us an early example of lack of congruence in the sg. verb and pl.

Right: The Böksta stone is now somewhat damaged but it no doubt depicts a hunting scene.
Left: The hunter is ready to let fly his arrow.

subject *Her skal standa stæinaʀ þessiʀ.* The reason is naturally first that the verb precedes the subject, and second that the expression more or less repeats a formula in which the sg. verb was normal.

It is not only in the poems of the *Edda* that runes play an important part. Scaldic poetry and sagas of Icelanders can also tell us much about their use. The best-known example of a poem recorded in runes is found in a famous episode in *Egils saga Skalla-Grímssonar*, where a poem of considerable length by Egil is said to have been cut on a wooden staff. This poem, the *Sonatorrek,* composed *c.* 960 according to the saga's chronology, is the most beautiful and most passionate of all scaldic poems.—Red-coloured runes are also mentioned several times. Such runes, correctly inscribed, saved Egil's life in a great drinking bout on Atley. He cut "ale-runes" in the horn to see whether his drink was poisoned. The runes he coloured with his own blood—*í dreyra*—and they caused the horn to break:

> *Rístum rún á horni,*   "We cut the rune on the horn,
> *rjóðum spjǫll í dreyra . . .*   redden the message in blood . . ."

Red runes also decided the fate of the outlaw, Grettir the Strong: runes which the sorceress, Þuríðr, cut on a tree-root and then coloured red were the cause of his death. She made part of one side of the root level and smooth: *síðan tók hon kníf sinn ok reist rúnar á rótinni ok rauð í blóði sínu ok kvað yfir galdra*—"then she took her knife and cut runes on the root and reddened them in her own blood and uttered spells over it".

Two other rune stones from Södermanland also say explicitly that they were painted. Thus, the inscription on one of the Gerstaberg stones in Ytterjärna

154

parish ends with the words: : **esbirn · risti · auk · ulfr · stainti** : *Æsbiorn risti ok Ulfʀ stæindi* "Äsbjörn carved and Ulv painted". The verb *stæina* (OWN *steina*, cf. English "stain, stained glass" etc.), "to paint, colour", was soon superseded by the loan-words *måla* (Low German *malen*) and *skriva* (Latin *scribere*)—the latter also had an original sense of "paint". We still find *stæina* used, however, in the verse romance *Konung Alexander,* composed at the end of the fourteenth century, where the sunlit sea is described as *faghert ok reent / som thet ware medh blomster steent* "as fair and pure as if it were painted with flowers". We may note too the eddaic poem, *Atlamál,* where Gudrun promises Atle a fitting burial: among other things she will buy him *kisto steinda* "a painted coffin".

Once upon a time the rune stones shone in bright colours, a remarkable addition to the beauty of the monuments. This stone from Öland is painted as it might have been originally.

The same word appears on the Nybble stone in Överselö parish which, as far as we can see, was carved by the Äsbjörn who signed the Gerstaberg stone. Here we meet the past part. adj. *stæindan:* **stain : hiuk : esbern : stintn : at : uitum : bat miþ : runum : raisti : kyla : at : gaiʀbern : boanta : sin : · auk · kofriþ : at : faþur : sin : han uaʀ : boanti : bestr i : kili : raþi : saʀ : kuni :**

Stæin hiogg Æsbern,	"Äsbjörn carved the stone,
stæindan at vitum,	coloured as a memorial,
bant með runum.	he bound it with runes.
Ræisti Gylla	Gylla raised it
at Gæiʀbern, boanda sinn,	after Gerbjörn, her husband,
ok Guðfrið at faður sinn.	and Gudfrid after his father.
Hann vaʀ boandi	He was the yeoman
bæztr i Kili.	best in Kil.
Raði saʀ kunni.	Let him read who can."

Painting of the carved surface is possibly also referred to on the Hogrän stone (Gotland): **: hier : mun : stanta stain : at : merki bietr a : bierki in bro furiʀ roþbiern risti : run[aʀ þ]esa kaiʀlaifʀ sumaʀ aʀ karla kan**

Hier mun standa	"Here shall stand
stainn at merki	the stone as a mark,
biæʀtr a bergi	bright on the rock,
en bro fyriʀ.	and the bridge in front.
Roðbiern risti	Rodbjörn cut
runaʀ þessaʀ,	these runes,
Gaiʀlaifʀ sumaʀ,	Gairlaiv some
eʀ garla kann.	who well knows how."

When the rune-master says the stone is **bie[r]tr a : bierki**, he may well be referring not merely to the pale surfaces of this magnificent monument but also to the bright colours with which the runes and ornament were painted. On another Gotland rune monument, the Ardre stones, traces of the original paint were still clearly visible.

An ancient connection between painting and runic writing is also demonstrated by the use of the verb *fa* (pret. *faði*). It originally meant "to paint", though it is evident that even in the earliest inscriptions it had already acquired a more general sense of "write" and is more or less synonymous with the verbs *writan* "write" and *wurkian* "work, make", which are also used in Primitive Norse inscriptions. *Fa* (< *faihian*) is still found in a few Viking Age inscriptions, but as a rule it has been replaced by the verbs *haggva* "hew, cut", *rista* "cut, incise", or *marka* "mark".

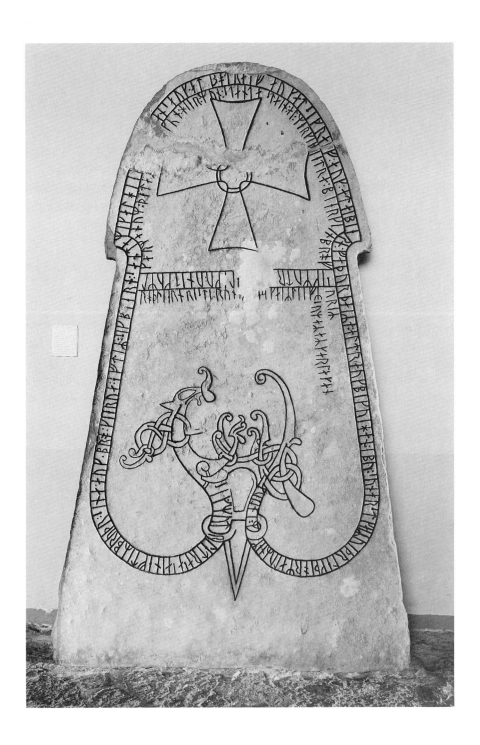

On the Hogrän stone from Gotland the Archangel Michael is invoked. Painting of the carved surface is possibly referred to in the text.

Two interesting illustrations of the custom of colouring incised runes can be culled from *Hávamál*. At one point in the poem, the rune-wise Odin says:

svá ek ríst	"so I cut
ok í rúnum fák...	and colour in the runes..."

— and in another place these questions are asked:

Veitstu, hvé rísta skal?	"Do you know how you shall cut?
Veitstu, hvé ráða skal?	Do you know how you shall read?
Veitstu, hvé fá skal?	Do you know how you shall paint?"

The oldest direct allusion to painted runes comes, however, from a source outside the Norse sphere. I refer to the well-known line by Venantius Fortunatus in a poem written towards the end of the sixth century:

Barbara fraxineis *pingatur* runa tabellis.
"The runes of the barbarians *are painted* on boards of ash."

These literary references to the painting of runes have, of course, their own special interest, but they cannot supply any detailed information about the appearance of monumental stones when fresh from the hands of the rune-master. Fortunately, a whole series of Swedish finds can now throw light on this hitherto obscure matter.

A number of rune stones have been discovered with their original colouring still on them. These stones have come to light in places where they have been protected for many centuries from sunshine and severe changes in weather. Most of them have been found embedded in the walls of medieval churches.

There is no doubt that the commonest colours used were red (red oxide of lead) and black (soot), although brown and white paints have also left definable traces.

In at least some cases it is clear that stones were painted in many colours. A find made in Köping church (Öland) in 1953–4 is especially noteworthy. Some sixty larger and smaller fragments were found, and they reveal that not only were the incised lines of the inscription picked out in colour but the intervening surfaces were also painted. This applies both to the ribbon along the edges of the stone, in which the runes themselves are enclosed, and to the coiling traceries within the inscribed lines. Further finds of painted stones, fragments of "Eskilstuna sarcophagi" (cf. p. 162 f. below), were made in 1959 and 1972 at Fors church (Eskilstuna) and in 1963 at Sundby church (Södermanland).

As for the painting of the runic inscription itself, the Köping find shows that sometimes colours were used alternately, so that the odd words were red, for

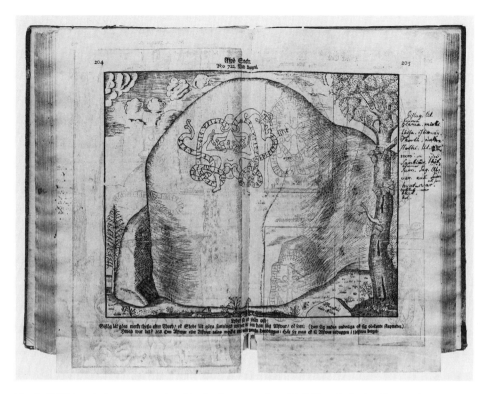

Nearly 1200 inscriptions are reproduced in the famous work entitled "Bautil, det är: alle svea ok götha rikens runstenar", published in 1750. The illustrations, chiefly drawn from the collection of Johan Hadorph (1630–93), were put together by the antiquarian Johan Göransson (1712–69). The one given here shows the Aspö carving (Södermanland), with a large human figure traced among the rune bands.

example, and the even words black. This method of indicating the division between words must have made it much easier to decipher the inscription. In one instance I have been able to demonstrate that the rune carver did not mechanically alternate his colours word by word, but used different colours for different parts of the sentence. When the subject comprised two words (*þæiʀ brøðr*), for example, the same colour was used for both, while the following predicate (*letu ræisa*), also comprising two words, had a different colour, and so on. The colouring thus served not only as an embellishment but as an effective guide to the sense. By painting in the runes, the writer also had an opportunity to correct errors he might have made with his chisel. If, for example, he had contrived to cut a ᚦ-rune instead of a ᚼ-rune, he would, after noticing his mistake, cut the correct diagonal stroke over the faulty letter. The result would then be an **h**-rune (ᚥ), but when he came to paint the inscription, he would pick out only the correct form of the rune and his error had vanished. There is one Uppland stone on which it can be shown that the end of the inscription was never cut at all, but only painted. That stone was carved by Öpir—a very productive rune-master but at times rather careless.

With stones carved in relief, it was probably most usual for the chiselled-out plane surfaces to be painted black, while the ribbon of runes and the ornamental traceries, which appeared in relief against this black background, were either painted in red or white or else left in their natural stone-colour.

We need have no doubt that people's love of colour in the Viking Age, attested as it is in so many ways, also found opulent expression on the rune stones. Painting brought out more clearly the intricate coils of the serpentine ornament and made the rune sequence easier to decipher.

The pride of the carvers and of the men and women who commissioned their work and their confident hope that the memory of the dead would be kept alive by their runes often find expression in the inscriptions:

> "Always shall stand
> while the stone lives
> this epitaph
> which Eskil carved."

The grand monument (*dyrð drængila, kumbl kenniligt*) will preserve the memory of a good man or woman

> "as long as the stone lives
> and the staves of the runes".

The inscription on this grave slab from St Hans church on Gotland says: Ever while the world wakes lies here over the man the memorial which his heir made in his memory.

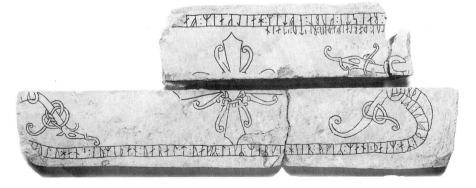

160

In 1982 a badly mutilated grave-slab was found in St Hans church in Visby (Gotland). Elegantly decorated in rune-stone style and inscribed with many runes, it was made about 1050 or, perhaps more probably, a decade or two later. In its message the inscription voices in this case an all too optimistic expectation that the memorial will escape the ravages of time. The ringing alliterative clauses may be reproduced thus in Runic Swedish:

> *æi meðan verald vakiʀ*
> *liggʀ mærki hiar yfiʀ manni þæim*
> *eʀ ærfingi æftiʀ gærði.*

"Ever while the world wakes lies here over the man the memorial which his heir made in his memory."

The rune-masters of the Viking Age sometimes succeeded in creating lasting monuments. The anticipation of the carver of the Runby block, for example, has—so far at least—proved true: his runes will remain, he says, "in memory of the men as long as mankind lives":

> *Þat skal at minnum manna*
> *meðan menn lifa.*

Runes from medieval and later times

With the end of the Viking Age, conditions of life grew more cramped than they had been for the yeomen-farmers and the young men of Sweden, and the custom of raising rune stones, in the proper sense, gradually died out. This does not of course mean that the use of runes came to an end. Runic writing has a long history in Sweden, a traditional practice that died hard.

Some inscriptions were described above (pp. 116 f.) which illustrate the great changes in social custom entailed in the burial of Christian men and women in consecrated ground. The last part of the eleventh century and all of the twelfth saw the erection of rune-inscribed monuments, often of a magnificent kind, in the church cemeteries.

The most impressive type among such monuments is that of the so-called Eskilstuna sarcophagi. They owe this name to the keen interest roused by the discovery of such a monument during excavations in 1912 on an early church-site in Eskilstuna.

The name is not a particularly happy one because, in fact, most later finds of such sarcophagi have been made elsewhere in Sweden, chiefly in Östergötland. But if this point is clearly appreciated, it is safe enough to retain the name as the general term for this important group of funerary monuments.

An Eskilstuna sarcophagus, then, consists of five stone slabs, two forming the sides, one the top, and two more the gable-ends; the last are sometimes shaped like a pointed arch, sometimes gently rounded. All five slabs may have carving on them, the gable stones usually on two sides. The runic inscriptions are frequently cut along the edges of these gables, and it is in these tall end-stones of the Eskilstuna sarcophagi that the rune-stone tradition lived on.

These sarcophagi are not coffins in the ordinary sense of the word. They were erected on top of the grave in which the corpse was laid, and were consequently never meant to enclose the body of the dead man. Any suggestion that the dead were left above ground in these magnificent edifices may be dismissed as unreasonable on grounds of hygiene alone.

These monuments, with handsome rune-stone ornament, often carved in relief, were painted in bright colours. Their splendour must have lent the graveyard an almost festive air.

In surmounting the grave as they did, these monuments resembled the various

This kind of sarcophagus is not a coffin in the ordinary sense of the word. It was erected on top of a grave. It consists of five slabs, which may all have carvings on them.

types of massive coffin-shaped stones that stood in the graveyards of Swedish churches in the early Christian period. A coffin-stone of this kind, consisting of a dressed block of redbrown sandstone, was discovered not long ago, in 1959, built into the wall of the church at Hammarby (Uppland). Evidently it must originally have lain in the churchyard there. The runic inscription runs along the four edges and reads: "Kristin had the memorial made for her son. Let everyone who reads the runes say prayers for Alle's soul. Sune was Alle's father."—×

krestin × let × glara × merki × eftiʀ × sun sen × huir sum runum riþr × hafi byniʀ × firiʀ × ala × sial × suni × uaʀ faþir × ala ×

This exhortation to say prayers for the soul of the dead person is found in a number of inscriptions. A grave-slab from Vamlingbo churchyard (Gotland), now lost, had almost exactly the same expression: **: hur : sum : runir : raþir : biþin : furi...** It also occurs, for example, on the Backgården stone in Bolum parish (Västergötland): *Svæinn Gislarssun let gæra bro þessa fyriʀ sial sina ok faður sins. Þat eʀ rett hværium at biðia Pater...* "Sven Gislarsson had this bridge made for his soul and his father's. It is right for everyone to say a Pater [noster]...". The inscription on a gravestone at Ukna (Småland) is in majuscules and runes, with the introduction and final prayer in Latin: HIC : IACET : TURGILLUS : **hærræ : guNmuNdæ : sun : gas : gak : ei : fra : stat : ok : sia : ok : læsin : lõrær : bøniʀ : firi : þyrhilsær : siæl : a : ve : ma : ria : graccia : ple : na : do : mi : nus : te : kum : benedikta : tu in mulieribus : æð benediktus : fruktus væntris : tui : amn : in manus tuas : d** "Hic iacet Turgillus, son of Herr Gudmund Gås. Go not hence, stay and see and read your prayers for the soul of Tyrgils! Ave Maria, gratia plena, Dominus tecum. Benedicta tu in mulieribus, et benedictus fructus ventris tui. Amen. In manus tuas D[omine commendo spiritum meum]." The Ukna slab, probably made *c.* 1300, is written in a fully dotted runic alphabet.

The use of prayer formulas of the kinds noted above was widespread and long-lived. The runic inscription on an Icelandic gravestone from the fifteenth century urges everyone who reads it to pray for the "blithe soul" of the dead and to sing the "blessed verse":

> *Hver er letrið les,*
> *bið fyrir blíðri sál,*
> *syngi signað vers.*

Among coffin-shaped gravestones the Vrigstad monument (Småland) deserves notice. It is furnished with gable-stones but is otherwise of the same type as the Hammarby stone.

The Ugglum stone (Västergötland) represents a younger type. It bears this verse-inscription, cut in relief: ✢ **þrir : liggia : mœnn : undir : þœmma : ✢ ✢ stene : gunnarr : sihvatr : hallstenn ✢** "Three men lie under this stone—Gunnar, Sigvat, Hallsten."

Like rune stones of the usual kind, these monuments we have just discussed were made and inscribed as memorials to dead kinsmen. There are many other medieval runic inscriptions, however, which did not serve this purpose.

It might be thought that the medieval church would not in general provide a congenial home for the custom of runic writing, but in fact we know many ecclesiastical objects with runes on them: baptismal fonts, reliquaries, the handsome iron-work of church-doors, bells, as well as inscriptions on the plaster of walls and on church-porches. The native runic writing which people could understand was clearly often preferred to the roman script of the learned.

In some cases a runic inscription tells us who built the church. Thus, it is from a rune stone that we learn about the builders of the church at Norra Åsum (Skåne): **+ krist : mario : sun : hiapi : þem : ær : kirku : þe... [g]erþ[o] : absalon : ærki : biskup : ok : æsbiorn muli** "Christ, Mary's son, help those who built this church, Archbishop Absalon and Äsbjörn Muzzle."

This coffin-shaped grave stone from Vrigstad's church in Småland is also furnished with gable-stones.

Of these two men, Archbishop Absalon may be fittingly described as one of the greatest and most impressive personalities in the history of medieval Scandinavia. He was the leading statesman in Denmark in the turbulent decades after 1150 and became archbishop of Lund in 1178. Since the inscription gives him his primate's title, it was clearly written after this latter date. Absalon died in 1201. It cannot be said for sure whether the inscription was made before or after his death, but it may seem reasonable to believe that it was in fact done while both he and his fellow-builder, Äsbjörn Muzzle, were still alive. Äsbjörn, we know, was a close associate of Absalon, but we are ignorant of the date of his death: it was probably before 1215.

Seen from the point of view of general cultural history, the fact that the memorial took the form of a rune stone must be of interest. It is surprising, to say the least, that a stone of this kind was set up as late as *c.* 1200—nearly 200 years, that is, after people in Skåne gave up carving rune stones in the old way. The explanation is probably to be sought in the archbishop's enthusiasm for the past and its relics. For Absalon the rune stone at Norra Åsum church can be counted an appropriate and significant monument.

An eleventh-century rune stone bears early witness to the existence of a church-builder in Lund. The stone was found in Södergatan and moved from there to be built into the wall of the bishop's palace in Copenhagen. The stone has lost its top and its inscription is unfortunately defective: **tuki : let : kirkiu : kirua : auk : . . .** "Toke had the church built and...". We cannot tell which church it was, and for us Toke is no more than a name.

Two Norwegian inscriptions deserve mention at this point. One of the inscriptions on the Oddernes stone in Vest-Agder says **ayintr × karþi × kirkiu × þisa × kosunr × olafs × hins × hala × a oþali × sinu** "Öjvind made this church, godson of St Olav, on his patrimonial estate". (In **kosunr** *goðsunr* we find the same loss of *ð* before *s* as in many Swedish runic spellings: **kus muþiʀ** *Guðs moðiʀ*, **kus : þaka** *Guðs þakka*.)

A marble tablet inserted in the wall above the altar in Tingvoll church in Nordmøre has this long and well-composed inscription: **+ ek : biþ : firi : guþrs : sakar : yþr : lærþa : menn : er uarþuæita : staþ : þænna : ok : alla : þa : er : raþa kunnu bøn : mina : minnizk : salo : minnar : i hælgum : bønom : en ek : et : gunnar : ok : gærþi : ek : hus : þætta + ualete** "I beg for God's sake you clergy who have charge of this church-place and all who can read my petition: remember my soul in your holy prayers. And I was called Gunnar and I made this house. Farewell!" The inscription can be dated to the beginning of the thirteenth century.

The runes which adorn the choir portal in Hellvi church (Gotland) were cut about 1300: **lafranz botuiðarsun maistera gerði kirkiu þisa : af yskilaim** "Lafrants, son of Master Botvid, made this church. From Eskelhem". It was thus Master Botvid, a well-known church-builder, who was Lafrants's father. The last two words, **af yskilaim** *af Yskilhaim*, are undoubtedly to be taken as a contraction:

From the inscription on this rune stone we learn about the builders of Norra Åsum church.

"They were (are) from Eskelhem."—Another long inscription in Anga church (Gotland) is painted on the north wall of the nave; it tells us of the yeomen-farmers who took part in the work on the church.

In some instances we find the names of stone-masons preserved in runes. Vallentuna church is of granite with a string of dressed sandstone quoins in the tower. On three of the sandstone blocks on the north side we are told who fashioned it: **andur : telhti þinna fakra sten :**... "Andor dressed this handsome stone". Looking at the quoins, we can well understand the mason's pride in his work.—On another sandstone block from Vallentuna the mason has left his name: **dafiþ** "David".—Vallentuna church is thought to have been built towards the end of the twelfth century, and since the tower belongs to its first stage we are given a welcome indication of the date of these two inscriptions in the dotted runic alphabet. The OSw. verb *tælghia,* OWN *telgja,* meant *i.a.* "dress, square, cut to shape"; it was used of timber as well as stone.

By far the finest of all rune fonts is the one at Åkirkeby, carved by the Gotlander, Sigraf. This masterpiece of the Gotland stonemason's art is in romanesque style and can be dated on stylistic grounds to the end of the twelfth century. Scenes from the life of Christ, from the Annunciation to the Crucifixion, are carved in relief in its eleven arcaded panels. At the top of each panel an inscription in dotted Gotlandic runes indicates the subject of the carving. The whole inscription is thus very long, containing over 400 runes: **þita : iʀ : saNti gabrel : ok : sehþi : saNta maria : at han skuLdi : barn : fyþa : þita : iʀ : elizabeþ : ok : maria : ok : hailsas : hiar : huilis : maria sum : han : barn : fydi : skapera : himiz : ok : iorþaʀ : sum os : leysti þita : iʀu : þaiʀ : þriʀ : kunuɢaʀ : sum : fyrsti : giarþu : ofr : uarum : drotNi : hiar : tok : haN : [uiþ]r : [kunuɢ]a : ofri : uar drotin hiar : riþu : þaiʀ : burt : þriʀ kunuɢaʀ : siþan þaiʀ : ofrat : hafa : orum · drotNi þaiʀ : þet : hiar : fram : s- -u : ioþar : toku uarn : drotin : ok... N : uiþr tre : ok : getu siþan : ladu : þaiʀ : haN : burt : þiaþaN : buNdiN ok : nehidu : hiar : ioþaʀ : iesus : a krus : si : fram : a þita sihrafʀ : [m]e[st]e[ri]** "This is St Gabriel who told St Mary that she would bear a child.—This is Elizabeth and Mary who greet each other.—Here Mary rests when she bore the child, the creator of heaven and earth, who redeemed us.—These are the three kings who first made offerings to Our Lord.—Here Our Lord received the offering of the kings.—Here they rode away, the three kings, after they hade made offerings to our Lord. Here they presented (?) it.—The Jews took Our Lord and scourged (?) him against the pillar and watched over him.—Afterwards they led him away from there bound.—And here the Jews nailed Jesus on the cross.—Look on this. Master Sigraf [made the font.]"

Linguistically and runologically the inscription is of surpassing interest. The Gotlandic fully dotted runic alphabet is used, a script skilfully adapted to match the phonetics of Gotland speech. It may

Above: The inscription on the Burseryd font reads: Arinbjörn made me. Vidkunn the priest wrote me. And here I shall stand for a while. *Below:* An inscription scratched in the plaster of the chancel arch in Björkeberg church says "This is the place of those who chant, not of others".

be noted that the yʀ-rune has its old value, ʀ. This is because Gotlandic retained the distinction between the palatal ʀ-sound and the usual tongue-tip dental *r* until well on in the middle ages. In a dozen positions Sigraf uses a dotted **n**-rune (ᛉ) represented here by **N**; a dotted **l**-rune (ᛁ) occurs once (here given as **L**). The rune reproduced as **G** has the form ᚤ and stands for the *ng*-sound. For *g* Sigraf has the ordinary dotted **g**-rune ᚦ.

A much simpler kind of font is found at Norum (Bohuslän), probably made in the early twelfth century. One reason why it claims attention is that below the runic inscription **suæn : kærþe m [lk]** "Sven made me" there is a picture of Gunnar in the snake-pen, playing his harp with his feet. This motif, one that was extremely tenacious of survival in the pictorial art of Scandinavia, was discussed on pp. 146 f. above.—The Hemsjö font (Västergötland) has this inscription: **alar**

The person who wrote the runes on this cross from Visby appeals to the women who followed Jesus to Jerusalem and kept watch at his tomb.

sialar : hær dopazs i ⫶ þiuþ ⫶ føri : mik ⫶ skal "All souls are here baptised into the congregation through me, the bowl".—The inscription on the Hossmo font (Småland) appeals to the reader with these words: **iak : biþ : þik : ... : at : þu : biþ nafnleka : fyrer : þæn : man : sum : mik : giorþe : iakob : het : han** "I pray you... that you pray by name for the man who made me. He was called Jakob".—Finally, the inscription on the beautiful font at Burseryd (Småland) intimates the evanescence of all that is mortal: **: arinbiorn ⫶ gørthe ⫶ mik ⫶ uitkunder ⫶ prester : skref : mik : ok ⫶ hær ⫶ skal : um ⫶ stund ⫶ stanta ⫶** "Arinbjörn made me. Vidkunn the priest wrote me. And here I shall stand for a while".

The numerous runic inscriptions on the walls of our churches can be represented here by only a couple of examples. A few years ago an inscription was

A chandelier from Väte church on Gotland. It has a runic inscription on an iron band riveted to its upper circlet.

found scratched in the plaster of the chancel arch in Björkeberg church (Öster-götland), thus marking the important boundary between the part of the church belonging to the people and the part belonging to the clergy. It says: · **hik** ⫶ **lokus** ⫶ **illorum** ⫶ **kui** ⫶ **kantant** ⫶ **non** · **aliorum** ⫶ "This is the place of those who chant, not of others". As we see, this has rhyme, like some lines painted in the choir of Film church (Uppland):

> *Rustice buck,*
> *quis te tulit huc?*
> *Est locus illorum*
> *qui cantant et non aliorum.*

"Rustic buck, who brought you here? It is the place of those who chant and not of others." (We remember that "choir" means both a body of singers and the place in church—the chancel—where they sing; the two are distinguished as *kör* and *kor* in Swedish.)

On the whole it comes as a surprise to find so many extant inscriptions using runes but written in Latin. So far over eighty have come to light in Sweden. As an example we may take a lead cross found in the Botanical Gardens in Visby in 1976. This little cross, only just over five cm tall, proved to be covered with runes. The long inscription has in fact nearly 100 runes and was probably written *c.* 1300. The writer appeals to the women who followed Jesus to Jerusalem and kept watch at his tomb. He begs them to intercede for the living: **intesede pro nobis semper : þ : sancta maria mater iacobi apostuli :þ: sancta maria maggalena :þ: salumee :þ: sancta caeri.**

Another example is the spindle-whorl discovered a few years ago at Brunflo in Jämtland, on the old road followed by pilgrims to St Olav's shrine in Nidaros (Trondheim). It is made of soapstone and incised with handsome, confident runes, just on a centimetre tall:

·⫶· **pahsportanti** ⫶ **salusabænti** ⫶ **ingiualtr** *Pax portanti, salus habenti, Ingevaldr.*
"Peace to the bearer! Safety to the owner! Ingevald."

Mural inscriptions are particularly common in Gotland churches. These runes are painted in red in Vänge church:

bedin · fyri · iakobs · sial · nikkarfua · han · do · fæm · daha fyri · sante · lafranz · dag ta · uar · f · sundahr · ok · m · primstafu-r · i · fimtanda ratu

"Pray for the soul of Jakob in Nickarve. He died five days before St Lawrence's day. Then (the rune) **f** was the Sunday letter and (the rune) **m** the "prime-stave" in the fifteenth row (of the Easter table)." This is typical of such Gotlandic inscriptions and presents no difficulties: the feast of St Lawrence is on 10 August; the fifteenth row of the Easter table covers the years 1532—59; the year in that sequence when the rune **f** was the Sunday letter and **m** the "prime-stave" was 1553: so Jakob Nickarve died on 5 August 1553.

A chandelier which was once suspended in Väte church on Gotland has finely inscribed runes on an iron band riveted to the chandelier's upper circlet. The band is unfortunately broken and the latter part of the inscription lost. As far as we can tell, both chandelier and inscription belong to the period around 1300: **+ iuan : i : grenium : han : gaf.·. þisa : krunnu : fyrst : gudi : ok : uari : frru : ok : þairi : helhu : kirkiu : senni : sial : til : þarfa ok : sida...** "Johan in Gräne, he gave this chandelier first to God and Our Lady and Holy Church for his soul's need, and then..."

Medieval church-bells were often inscribed with runes and we know more than twenty such in Sweden. Bells were after all "christened" when they were consecrated, and it was in that way, at the time of its consecration in the thirteenth century, that the Bollebygd bell (Västergötland) came by the name of Katerina, as we learn from the Leonine hexameters written in two ribbons of runes on the bell's exterior: **+ dat : kterina : sonum : / fideli : populo : bonum + / + ik : sonus : auditur : / ik : mens : turbata : blandidur** "Katerina gives a sweet sound to faithful people. Here the sound is heard; here a troubled mind is calmed".

Even as late as in the sixteenth century runes were still used on the often very grand gravestones adorning the cemeteries of Gotland. Sometimes they have both a Latin inscription in roman capitals and a vernacular one in runes. The position of runes as a popular script was clearly well maintained, and indeed a study of these latterday inscriptions gives the impression that in some parts of Sweden the ordinary people found the roman alphabet quite foreign throughout the middle ages. In 1611 Johannes Bureus—who admittedly was born in Uppland and was to become both State Antiquary and State Archivist—published his runic ABC, a book evidently intended for use in schools. It was also planned to use runes instead of roman letters in printed books. In this way we should repair the harm done when, "as a result of the pope's power over Christ's infant flock", Latin script had ousted the Swedes' honourable and venerable runes.

Evidence that knowledge of runes lived on in full vigour can be drawn from many quarters, not least from the so-called rune staves. These were in almost universal use as calendars, with runes used for the calendar signs, dominical letters and so forth. Such runic calendars and calendar boards were still in use in the nineteenth century. Of the hundreds of them preserved in Nordiska Museet I shall select only one, the calendar from Gammalsvenskby in Russia. It is dated 1766 and must consequently have been made on Dagö (in Estonia) before the Swedish community there was forced to move to the Ukraine. And there for a

So-called rune staves were in almost universal use as calendars. Runes were used for calender signs, dominical letters and so forth. Such runic calendars were still in use in the nineteenth century.

century and a half in the depths of south Russia people kept watch on the passage of time with the aid of the rune calendar from Dagö. It was brought to Stockholm by a member of the Gammalsvenskby community in 1900.

When Carl von Linné reached Älvdalen on his journey through Dalarna in 1734 he wrote in his diary: "The peasants in the community here, apart from using rune staves, still today write their names and ownership marks with runic letters, as is seen on walls, corner stones, bowls, etc. Which one does not know to be still continued anywhere else in Sweden." It is obvious that the tradition behind runic writing in Dalarna is ancient, but so far the oldest *dated* inscription comes from Åsen in Älvdalen: "Anders has made (this) bowl anno 1596". The custom of using runes for notes and messages of various kinds has continued in Älvdalen almost to our own time. An inventory of runic inscriptions in Dalarna, now in progress, has listed over 200, most of them cut in wood. They are found on a variety of household articles, on bowls, bridal boxes, furniture and kitchen blocks, on the buildings of shielings, on sticks recording the size of land-plots (the sticks are called *revstickor* because a line—*rev*—was used for the measuring) —and so on. Usually they are brief but occasionally longer texts are found. The inscription on the handsome milk-bowl from Hykie may be cited as an example: **mas : iendeson hafver : giort : thena skål : en : hyke : bye datum then : 9 : septemberh : ugit : i : päs : graf : utaf : stuuben ano : År MDCCIV : å : giud gifve : at : hon : vil : våara ful : oc : aldrigh : gieärna tom : mädh : goda : skiöna oc : siöta : flötor : sä vore : thä : mykit väl** "Mats Hindersson has made this bowl at Hykie hamlet datum 9 September, cut in Persgrav from the stump anno the year 1704. Ah, God give it may ever be full and never readily empty of good, lovely and fresh cream. Then it would be very fine."

The bog-iron smelter Jugås Erik Olsson from Månsta in Älvdalen inscribed this message on the bottom of his bowl: E O S 1749 **dena : skålen : afuer : iag / giort : första : ååret : iag / blåste : norde : i : sleskian : ok / då : slute : uii : blåsa : den : 16 oktober.** "E O S 1749 I have made this bowl in the first year I smelted north in *Sleskian* and we then stopped smelting on 16 October."

One of the longest known inscriptions from Älvdalen was found in 1960 in Brunnbergs by in connection with the inventory. The inscription, cut on a staff, tells how the writer and another man from Älvdalen "marched to Stockholm in two weeks", arriving on 20 June. There they were "taken as prisoners" and they stayed in captivity "for a month or until 20 July". Afterwards they were allowed "to march under guard" home to Älvdalen again. The inscription thus gives a contemporary account of the revolt in Dalarna in 1743—that is, of the grave crisis when Dala-men embarked on *Stora daldansen*—"the great ball of the Dala-men"—and marched to defeat in Stockholm.

The province of Dalarna has rightly been called "the last stronghold of the Germanic script".

That the use of runes lasted so long in remoter parts of Sweden can be seen as a sign of the firm grip this antique Germanic system of writing had on us. On the chancel-wall of Runsten church (Öland) there was once the following runic inscription: *tæt bør soknahærræn kunnæ runær læsæ och skrivæ* "The pastor of the parish should know how to read runes and write them". This was composed by the parson of the parish himself, about the middle of the sixteenth century. One has the feeling that he was voicing the demands made on him by the ordinary folk in his flock.

From time to time we Swedes make our unique wealth in runic inscriptions a matter of pride and glory, but these riches can also give rise to reflections of a less self-congratulatory nature. We loyally went on using the script inherited from our forefathers. We clung tenaciously to our runes, longer than any other nation. And thus our incomparable abundance of runic inscriptions also reminds us of how incomparably slow we were—slow and as if reluctant—to join the company of the civilised nations of Europe.

Bibliography and notes

Most of the runic inscriptions mentioned in this book are discussed in greater detail in the volumes of *Sveriges runinskrifter*—the enterprise known as Runverket (a term also used of the institute responsible for it)—published by the Royal Academy of Letters, History and Antiquities (Vitterhetsakademien). The provinces so far covered are represented by these volumes: *Gotlands runinskrifter* I–II (1962–78; a third and final volume is expected in a couple of years); *Gästriklands runinskrifter* (1981); *Närkes runinskrifter* (1975); *Smålands runinskrifter* (1935–61); *Södermanlands runinskrifter* (1924–36); *Upplands runinskrifter* (1940–58; a supplement and introductory survey are in progress); *Värmlands runinskrifter* (1978); *Västergötlands runinskrifter* (1940–70); *Västmanlands runinskrifter* (1964); *Ölands runinskrifter* (1900–06); and *Östergötlands runinskrifter* (1911–18). Work on the publication of *Hälsinglands runinskrifter* has begun, and Runverket has embarked on preliminary investigations into the material from the remaining provinces.

It should be mentioned that the first volumes of *Sveriges runinskrifter*, those on Öland and Östergötland published at the beginning of the century, are now out of date. To a large degree this is because of the numerous new finds made in recent decades, in these provinces as elsewhere. Runverket is superintending the collection of material for new modern editions of these volumes. Many newly discovered, or rediscovered, runic inscriptions have been published over the years in *Fornvännen* (Tidskrift för svensk antikvarisk forskning; published by Vitterhetsakademien), and information about new finds will continue to appear in this journal.

For information about inscriptions in Skåne, Halland and Blekinge reference should, for the present, be made to *Danmarks Runeindskrifter* (1941–42), and to Erik Moltke, *Runerne i Danmark og deres Oprindelse* (1976), which is now in English, with some additional material, as *Runes and their Origin: Denmark and Elsewhere* (1985). The Bohuslän inscriptions have been published in the Norwegian series, *Norges innskrifter med de yngre runer* 5 (1960), 220–30.

Inscriptions published in the volumes of Runverket are referred to by abbreviations in which the initial letter or letters indicate the volume according to province and the following figure the number of the inscription in the volume, thus: G = *Gotlands runinskrifter*, Gs = *Gästriklands runinskrifter*, Nä = *Närkes runinskrifter*, Sm = *Smålands runinskrifter*, Sö = *Södermanlands runinskrifter*, U = *Upplands runinskrifter*, Vg = *Västergötlands runinskrifter*, Vr = *Värmlands runin-skrifter*, Vs = *Västmanlands runinskrifter*, Ög = *Östergötlands runinskrifter*, Öl = *Ölands runinskrifter*. The Danish runic corpus is abbreviated DR, the Norwegian NIyR.

The three large-scale Scandinavian series contain detailed references to the relevant scholarly literature. Their amplitude allows me to limit my references to a number of more recent publications and to works of importance either in considering specific problems or in discussing general theoretical approaches.

Among runological surveys may be mentioned: E. Brate, *Sveriges runinskrifter* (2nd ed., 1928); O. von Friesen, *Upplands runstenar* (1913), *Runorna i Sverige* (1928), *Runorna* (in *Nordisk Kultur* 6, 1933); W. Krause, *Runeninschriften im älteren Futhark* (2nd ed., 1966); E. Moltke. *Runerne i Danmark og deres oprindelse* (1976; in English as *Runes and their Origin: Denmark and Elsewhere,* 1985); L. Musset, *Introduction à la runologie* (1965); K. Düwel, *Runenkunde* (2nd ed., 1983); R. Elliott, *Runes* (1959); R.I. Page, *An Introduction to English Runes* (1973); A. Ruprecht, *Die ausgehende Wikingerzeit im Lichte der Runeninschriften* (1958); Niels Å. Nielsen, *Danske Runeindskrifter* (1983).

NOTES

p. 9   For contributions to the discussion on the origin of runes see e.g. O. von Friesen, Runorna (1933) 5f., with references; E. Moltke, Runerne i Danmark (1976), Runes and their Origin: Denmark and Elsewhere (1985); L. Musset, Introduction à la runologie (1965); W. Krause, Die Runeninschriften im älteren Futhark (1966) 6f.

p. 10   The great antiquity of runes was maintained for example by the learned Johannes Magnus, the last Catholic archbishop to reside in Sweden. In his grandiose and in many respects admirable Historia de omnibus Gothorum Sveonumque regibus, printed in Rome in 1554, he wrote: "The Göter had their letters and writings long before the Latin were invented"—as is shown by "the great stones erected by the ancient graves and cemeteries of the Göter. Letters are cut on these stones from which we may readily learn that they were erected by mighty heroes before the Flood or immediately after it."

p. 11   The Gårdlösa brooch: The inscription is misunderstood in the book O forna tiders kvinnor (Statens Historiska Museer, 1975) 89.

p. 12   On the futhark sequence, division into "families" and names of runes see e.g. O. von Friesen, Runorna (1933) 35f.

p. 25   On the 16-rune futhark: E. Wessén, Om vikingatidens runor (Filologiskt arkiv 6; 1957), Från Rök till Forsa (Filologiskt arkiv 14; 1969); E. Moltke, Runerne i Danmark (1976), Runes and their Origin: Denmark and Elsewhere (1985).

p. 26   The Novgorod bone piece: I. Sanness Johnsen, Stuttruner (1968) 169.

p. 28   Staveless runes: S.B.F. Jansson, De stavlösa runornas tydning (Filologiskt arkiv 30; 1983).

p. 29   The inscriptions in Bergen: A. Liestøl, Runer frå Bryggen (in Viking 27; 1964), Runic voices from towns of ancient Norway (in Scandinavica 13; 1974).
On medieval runology in Sweden see E. Svärdström in Rig 1972, 77f., Runfynden från gamla Lödöse (1982).

p. 31   The Sparlösa stone: Vg 119; the Rök stone: Ög 136; E. Wessén, Runstenen vid Röks kyrka (Vitterhetsakademiens handlingar, Filologisk-filosofiska serien 5; 1958), Rök, ett fornminne och ett ortnamn (in Fornvännen 1975, 5f.), Från Rök till Forsa (Filologiskt arkiv 14; 1969). O. Grønvik, Runeinnskriften på Rök-steinen (in Maal og minne 3–4, 1983, 101–149)

p. 37   The Oklunda inscription: A Nordén, Ett rättsdokument från en fornsvensk offerlund (in Fornvännen 1931, 330f.); O.v. Friesen, Runorna (1933) 152f.
The Forsa ring: A. Liestøl, Runeringen i Forsa (in Saga och Sed 1979, 12f.).

p. 39   The Kälvesten stone: A. Nordén, "Sparlösa" och "Kälvesten", våra äldsta historiska runinskrifter (in Fornvännen 1961, 256f.).

p. 47   The Ladoga inscription: G. Høst, Innskriften fra Gamle Ladoga (in Norsk tidsskrift for sprogvidenskap 19, 1960, 418f.); W. Krause, Die Runeninschrift von Alt-Ladoga (ibid., 555f.); A. Liestøl, Runic Inscriptions (in Varangian Problems, 1970, 122f.), The Literate Vikings (in Proceedings of the Sixth Viking Congress [Uppsala 1969], 1971, 70).

p. 54   Asmundr Karason: S.B.F. Jansson, Runristare (in Kulturhistoriskt lexikon för nordisk medeltid 14, 1969, col. 497f.).

p. 60   The Gårdby stone: Öl 28; S.B.F. Jansson, Till tolkningen av Gårdbystenen på Öland (in Arkiv för nordisk filologi 62, 1947, 186).

p. 61   The Berezanj stone: T.J. Arne, Den svenska runstenen från ön Berezanj utanför Dnjepermynningen (in Fornvännen 1914, 44f.).

p. 62   The Piræus lion: H. Shetelig, Piræus-löven in Venezia (in Fornvännen 1923, 201f.); E. Brate, Yttrande över föregående arbete (in Fornvännen 1923, 222f.); S.B.F. Jansson, Pireuslejonets runor (in Nordisk tidskrift 1984, pt. 1).

p. 63   On the Ingvar stones: G. Jarring, Serkland (in Namn och Bygd 1983, 125f.); M. Larsson, Vart for Ingvar den vittfarne? (in Fornvännen 1983, 95f.).

p. 90   The Högby stone: Ög 81; Th. Andersson, Högbystenens runinskrift (in Festskrift till Olav Ahlbäck, 1971, 17f.) with references.

p. 100   The Malsta stone: O. v. Friesen in Runorna (1933) 160f.; S.B.F. Jansson, De stavlösa runornas tydning (Filologiskt arkiv 30; 1983); Två runstenar i Hälsingland: Malsta och Sunnå (Filogogiskt arkiv 33; 1985).

p. 108   The two rune stones at the south end of Jarlabank's bridge were moved before the Reformation, one to Danderyd church, the other to Fresta church.

p. 111   Rune stone with the phrase *gæra aur*: T. Holmberg, Göra ör efter sina söner (in Fornvännen 1974, 202f.).

p. 112   "Die in white clothes": on the rune stone found in 1972 see Fornvännen 1973, 192f.

p. 114   Vg 186: Timmele churchyard, now at Dagsnäs.

p. 115   Vg 105: Särestad's old church.

           Vg 122: Abrahamstorp, Barne-Åsaka, now at Dagsnäs.

p. 121   The Jarlabanke stone at Vallentuna church: U 212; Th. Andersson, Iarlabanki atti alt hundari þetta (in Svenska studier från runtid till nutid, 1973, 16f.).

p. 128   The Hassmyra stone: Vs 24; L. Peterson, Kvinnonamnens böjning i fornsvenskan (Anthroponymica suecana 8; 1981) 149.

p. 129   The Härene stone: Vg 59; E. Salberger, Sum:kuin (in Arkiv för nordisk filologi 19, 1975, 111f.).

p. 133   *Þorbiorn skald*: U 25, 532.

           GrimR skald: U 951 and probably U 916.

           Uddr skald: Vg 4.

p. 137   *i grati*: Jón Helgason, Bällsta-inskriftens "i grati" (in Arkiv för nordisk filologi 59, 1944, 159f.).

p. 138   Maeshowe nr 18: M. Olsen, De norröne runeinnskrifter (in Runorna, Nordisk Kultur 6, 1933, 102f.).

p. 141   The Ribe stick: E. Moltke, Runepindene fra Ribe (in Fra Nationalmuseets Arbejdsmark 1960, 122f.).

p. 145   The Ramsund carving: Sö 101. Another interesting depiction of Sigurd slayer of Favner is in Hyllestad church in Norway, see W. Holmqvist, Germanic art (1955), pl. 62; M. Blindheim, Norwegian romanesque decorative sculpture 1090–1210 (1965), pl. 197–8.

p. 147   The Oseberg cart: A.W. Brøgger and H. Shetelig, The Viking ships (1951) 92.

p. 148   The Franks Casket: in Runorna (Nordisk Kultur 6, 1933) 50f.; J. Beckwith, Ivory Carvings in Early Medieval England (1972), Cat. no. 1.

p. 152   Kirk Andreas (Man): P.M.C. Kermode, Manx Crosses (1907) 192 and pl. 52; S.M. Margeson in The Viking Age in the Isle of Man (1983) 95f.

p. 158   The Köping find: S.B.F. Jansson, Om runstensfynden vid Köping på Öland (in Fornvännen 1954, 83f.).

p. 164   A gravestone from Grenjaðarstaður (Iceland): A. Bæksted, Islands Runeindskrifter (1942) 176f.

p. 173   Rune staves: S.O. Jansson, Runkalendarium (in Kulturhistoriskt lexikon för nordisk medeltid 14, 1969, col. 494f., with references).

Index of inscriptions

Numbers in italics refers to illustrations

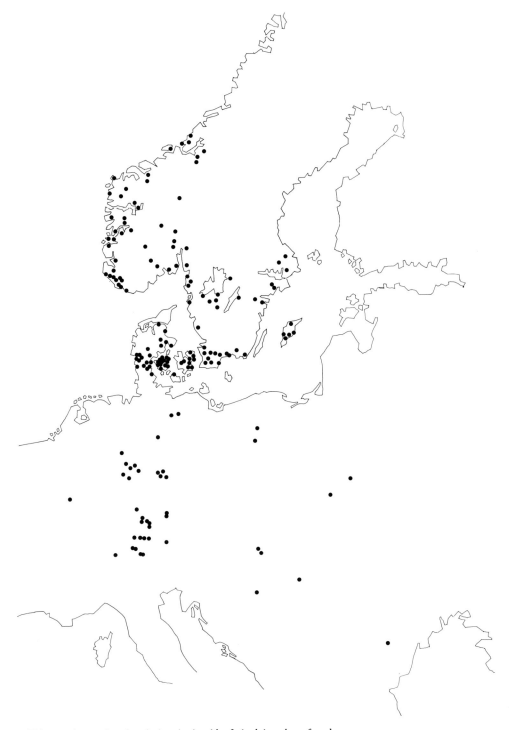

This map shows where inscriptions in the older futhark have been found.

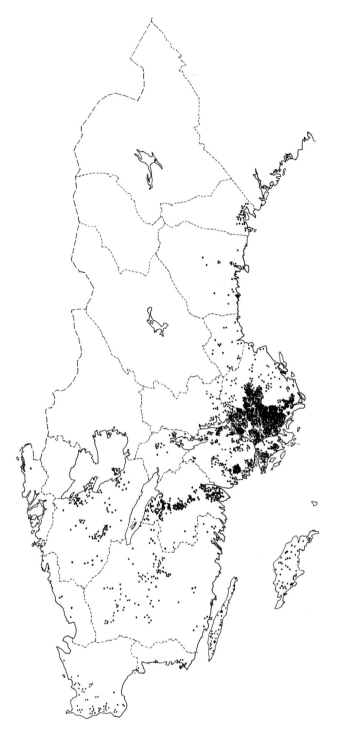

A distribution-map showing Viking Age inscriptions in the 16-symbol futhark. Their chief concentration in the Mälar region is obvious.